Cooking with Beer

'IF THERE'S LIQUID IN A RECIPE, IT MIGHT AS WELL BE BEER'

Cooking with Beer

'IF THERE'S LIQUID IN A RECIPE, IT MIGHT AS WELL BE BEER'

Paul Mercurio

MURDOCH BOOKS

Contents

Welcome!

Beer has always been seen as a man's drink. It's what the blokes drink around the barbecue as they overcook the steaks while the women are inside sipping chardonnay and making the salads. It's what blokes chug back after mowing the lawn, or use to wash down a pie and sauce at the footy. These great cultural pleasures have been enjoyed for many a year, and long may they live – however, times are changing and it is my hope that this book will help to drive the changes even faster.

Thankfully it's no longer unusual to go to a bar, a pub or a backyard barbecue and see a group of people – men and women – all drinking beer. What is unusual is the range of beers they may be drinking; the guys might be drinking amber ale, English bitter, a double India pale ale or a Belgian wit and the women might be enjoying a Kölsch, a sparkling ale or an Austrian pilsner. On the menu will be anything gourmet – from sausages, pizza, terrines or paella to weird and wonderful dips and cheeses. We now have a wide variety of great produce available to us and that means people are now looking for, asking for and wanting flavour. In Australia we have well over one hundred micro-breweries around the country, all making great beers with their own unique flavours.

Beer has changed and so has the way people look at beer. It is no longer the cheap and relatively tasteless mega-swill that you drink just because your dad did and his dad before him. It is now a considered part of a dinner party, a family function or a good night out. Pubs and restaurants are now matching beers to the dishes on their menus – something the micro-breweries have been doing for years. Boutique bars serving only micro-brewed and specialty beers are springing up all over the country and beer dinners are starting to become commonplace.

Better still, the use of beer as a cooking ingredient has finally moved beyond the ubiquitous beer-battered fish and chips. Don't get me wrong, I love beer-battered fish and chips and have it often, but nowadays I match the beer in the batter to the fish or seafood I am cooking – a pilsner for prawns (shrimp), sparkling ale for flake, and stout for mussels or oysters. The combinations and possibilities are endless, and the world of beer and food is ... well, it's your oyster (Oyster Stout of course!).

Beer has finally come of age as a sophisticated beverage that both men and women are enjoying in greater numbers than ever before. It has a well-deserved and unique place on the table at home, in the restaurant, by the barbecue and in the dish being served.

When I told people I was writing a beer cookbook their general reaction was to say how much their husband, boyfriend or son would love it, and I hope they do – I hope wives, girlfriends and sisters buy it in the thousands for their loved ones. However, my aim in writing this book was to write it for men and women alike who share my love for a fine lager or ale and, importantly, for people who like good food. I have cooked all the dishes in this book and I have fed them to my wife, my daughters, my mum, my in-laws, my friends, my children's friends, my butcher, my bank manager, my bottle shop attendant and many others. I am glad to say they all loved the dishes!

The key to cooking with beer is to create really good dishes that stand on their own, are well balanced, well flavoured and don't taste like beer. If every dish in this book tasted like beer there would be no point in writing more than one recipe. Beer is but one ingredient and it must work in a harmonious and complementary way with all the other ingredients.

Beer in itself is a unique drink, but used as an ingredient in a recipe it will add all sorts of wonderful complexity to a dish. There are eighty-seven recognised beer

styles in the world, each with its own flavour profile and nuance. There are thousands of breweries around the globe making these styles, and each brewery has its own unique character that it imparts into their beers.

For instance, pilsner is the most prolific beer style and is made by almost every country in the world, but if you did a side-by-side tasting of pilsners from China, Japan, Austria, Australia, Canada, the United States, Malaysia and the Philippines, you would be amazed by the differences between them. Try a side-by-side tasting of Australian-made pilsners only and again you would be amazed at the differences. See what I mean about complexity? So when you use beer in your cooking you have an incredible amount of choice, subtlety and flavour profiles to experiment with. Therefore the key to making a really good dish is to choose an appropriate beer with the flavour nuances that will best suit the dish.

How best do you do this? Taste lots of beers! One size does not fit all, so there's no point in using your favourite beer in all the recipes in this book. You can if you want to – the recipes will work – but you will be missing out on some wonderful and unique characteristics brought to these recipes by the specific styles of beer I have used. Experiment and have fun – cooking with beer is an adventure and one I'm sure you will enjoy! I certainly do!

Cheers,

Paul

Beer 101
a quick overview

Beer is made using malted barley, hops, water and yeast. To those ingredients, depending on the style of the beer, you can add rice, corn, malted and unmalted wheat, different sorts of sugars, and even fruits. For instance the big Belgian high-alcohol style of beer often uses candy sugar to add to its flavour profile, and again in Belgium they add fruit to a special brew called a lambic to create a fruit-driven effervescent beer. Essentially you will find that your friendly boutique micro-brewer is sticking to the traditional method of using just the four main ingredients I mentioned first.

To make a beer you steep malted barley (grain) in warm water for about an hour – this is known as the 'mash'. The temperature of the water will affect the body quality and mouth-feel of the finished beer. During the mash the starches in the grain are converted into fermentable and non-fermentable sugars. Once this conversion has happened, the grain is rinsed (or 'sparged', in brewing talk) so that all the sugars in the grain are rinsed out, and the sparging liquid (now called 'wort' – pronounced wert) is then transferred to a kettle. (The spent grain from the mash is often picked up by farmers, who feed it to their cows.) The wort is boiled vigorously for about an hour, to get rid of any undesirables in the liquid that can cause problems with the beer later on. At various times throughout the boil, hops are added. Hops do several things for beer – they add aroma and flavour; they add bitterness; and they help to preserve the beer. There are more than seventy varieties of hops grown around the world, with more being developed every year. Each has its own distinctive flavour and character.

Once the wort has boiled for an hour and the hop additions have been made, the liquid is pumped through a chiller into a fermenter, where the yeast is added. The yeast's sole function is to eat the fermentable sugars in the wort. During this process the yeast produces vital by-products, excreting (for want of a better term) carbon dioxide and alcohol – this process is called fermentation and usually takes five to seven days depending on the beer you are making. Once fermentation is finished, the beer may or may not be filtered and pasteurised, depending on the brewery and the style of the beer, and then it is either bottled or put in kegs and is ready to drink.

Simple?

Well, not really. The brewing process is fairly straightforward, but when you realise that the brewer has to choose between the seventy-plus different hops, an equal amount of various malts and manufacturers and more than fifty-five different yeast strains, it becomes clear that making a good beer is not so simple. Juggling all those flavours is an art in itself.

The very large commercial breweries produce a fine product that is collectively known as mega-swill, meaning it is for the masses. To produce such a beer the big breweries take all sorts of measures (some might say shortcuts) to produce a beer that tastes the same with every brew and is cost efficient. To do this they add all sorts of adjuncts that don't really improve the flavour of the beer. Nor does the high proportion of cane sugar – up to 40 per cent and possibly more – which they often use. Among other things – as in the case of high-gravity brewing – they add the hops when they bottle! This to me is like serving the salt, pepper, carrots, celery and herbs for your stew on the side when you serve up. They also add rice, corn and other ingredients to give mouth-feel and to help with such things as head retention and colour. The result is a consistent and cost-effective brew – and personally I cannot stand it. Put simply, mega-swill is not suitable to cook with as it is not going to add

complexity, subtlety, flavour or any unique nuance to your dish. You will get a beery character but nothing else. For this reason I recommend that you do not cook with mega-swill, or for that matter with light beer.

So what beer should you cook with? Well, there are only two types of beer in the world – some would say good ones and bad ones, which I would agree with, although that is a very subjective and personal appraisal. In fact the two types of beer are lager and ale. All beer styles fall under these two headings. So under lagers you have lager, pilsner, bock, dunkel, schwarzbier and others, and under the umbrella of ale there are ale, pale ale, bitter, India pale ale, brown, stout, porter, wheat beers, lambics and others. There are more ale styles than lager styles – don't ask me why, although I suspect it is because ales have been around for a lot longer than lagers.

The difference between the two is how they are brewed. Lager is brewed with a yeast – often referred to as a lager yeast – that prefers a colder environment. The effect of this is to make a beer that is quite clean and uncomplicated. A lager may be brewed using one malt style and one hop style. Lagers are quite clear or bright, although they can vary from crystal clear to very dark. Because they are brewed at low temperatures they do not develop fruity characters but rather are clean, crisp, uncomplicated beers. Ales, on the other hand, are brewed at warmer temperatures with an ale yeast, which encourages the development of fruity esters. This gives ales a bigger mouth-feel and a more fruity character. Ales are also more complex beers, often using several malts and hop varieties in the one brew, which again gives them a much bigger profile in terms of mouth-feel, residual sugars, flavour, bitterness and aroma. For this reason I use ales in my cooking far more often than lagers.

My favourite style to cook with is wheat beer. To me it contributes a lovely silkiness to the flavour profile of a dish and the beers themselves have lots of unique character. The Belgian wit style is a wheat beer brewed with an addition of coriander (cilantro) and orange peel, while the traditional German hefeweizen wheat beers have strong hints of banana and cloves that come from the yeast. Both styles of beer are great in a diverse range of dishes from seafood risotto to chicken casseroles to all sorts of cakes.

I also love cooking with the big Belgian ale styles, which normally have a rather high alcohol content. In the same way that fat is flavour, so too is alcohol. To get a high alcohol content you need to use lots more malt, and in doing so the brewer needs to think much more carefully about balancing the beer out with hops and perhaps other adjuncts such as candy sugar. The resulting beer is magnificent and unique – the perfect late-night tipple with some farmhouse cheese, and even better as a brilliant component in a slow-cooked osso bucco or a dense and fragrant fruit cake.

The beers I have used for the recipes in this book are those that I love, I drink and I stand by as great beers which work well in the recipes – but importantly, they're those I can buy. There are other beers I've had that I would have loved to use in this book, brewed by award-winning breweries in Western Australia, New South Wales, New Zealand, Canada, the United States and other places, but I couldn't get them. There are great beers brewed all around the world and we are lucky that the large liquor chains and some boutique smaller ones are stocking a great selection of them, but sometimes the beer that tastes the best is being brewed just around the corner.

In these recipes I have given the beer style I have used in the dish and also the name of the beer I have used, with some possible alternatives, but really this is just a guide for you. I hope you will explore and use the beers lovingly brewed by your local micro-brewers.

Good with beer

I could have written a whole book on snacks that go well with beer – in fact I may just do that – but for now I've included some of my all-time favourite things to have with a beer. Some of them are quite simple, so you can whip them up really quickly and then enjoy them on your own, or with your loved one or a friend. Others do require a little more thought and preparation and are perfect on your own, but also work a treat if you're having a couple of friends around for a few lazy Sunday afternoon drinks. Even better, if you are having a big party, cook them all up a day or two ahead and you'll have an awesome array of great beer snacks which will really impress your guests. You can top all that quality cooking off by going to your local micro-brewery, hiring a keg and serving some great-quality handmade craft beer as well. Perfect!

Carrot and cumin dip

750 g (1 lb 10 oz) carrots, peeled, topped and tailed
2–3 tablespoons olive oil, plus 2–3 tablespoons extra
2 tablespoons honey (orange blossom is terrific)
1 teaspoon cumin seeds, dry-roasted in a frying pan over medium heat

3–4 garlic cloves, unpeeled
½ teaspoon ground coriander
1 teaspoon ground cumin
½ teaspoon ground ginger
¼ teaspoon cayenne pepper
juice of 1 lemon
1 tablespoon cream (optional)

Preheat the oven to 180°C (350°F/Gas 4). Cut the carrots in half crossways and then again lengthways. In a baking tin, dress the carrots with 2–3 tablespoons of the olive oil, then drizzle with the honey. Add the cumin seeds and garlic, season with freshly ground black pepper and toss well. Roast until the carrots are softened, but still a little firm in the middle, 20–25 minutes. Remove from the oven and put the carrots in a blender. Take the skin off the garlic and place the cloves in the blender also.

Add the ground spices and blend, gradually adding the lemon juice and then some extra olive oil. Lastly add the cream, if using. This dip should be a little chunky, which is why you shouldn't overcook the carrots, nor overblend them with the spices; add just enough oil to loosen the consistency of the dip, but don't make it too loose. Season to taste with salt and freshly ground black pepper.

Serve with fresh pide (Turkish/flat bread) and your favourite beer.

MAKES ABOUT 2 CUPS

When you buy a piece of corned silverside from your butcher, it usually comes in a vacuum-sealed packet and often weighs anywhere from 1.5 kg (3 lb 5 oz) to 2.5 kg (5 lb 8 oz). The amount of salt in the brine can also vary from butcher to butcher, depending on their recipe. As there is a fair amount of salt coming from the soy sauce in this recipe, you don't really want your silverside to be too salty. Unfortunately the only way to find out how salty the silverside will actually be is to buy it and try it. Once you find a butcher who makes silverside to your liking, do two things: tell him you like it and give him some of your jerky. A good relationship with your butcher is an important part of your culinary journey.

Homemade beef jerky

1 piece of corned silverside; choose a good
   lean one
125 ml (4 fl oz/½ cup) soy sauce or
   salt-reduced tamari
2 tablespoons worcestershire sauce
2 tablespoons Wild Turkey bourbon
1 teaspoon garlic powder

1 teaspoon smoked paprika
1 teaspoon onion powder
½ teaspoon ground ginger
1 teaspoon chilli powder
½ teaspoon cayenne pepper
1 tablespoon honey

Trim away all the fat and any skin membrane on your silverside. Cut the meat across the grain into steaks 3 cm (1¼ inches) thick. Freeze the steaks until they are partly frozen, then remove one from the freezer. (Having the steaks partly frozen makes it easier to cut nice, even, thin strips of meat.) Lay the steak down, with what was the top of the silverside facing the right side if you are right handed, or to the left if you are left handed. With a very sharp knife, cut slices 2–3 mm (1/16–1/8 inch) thick from the steak. (Cutting along from what was the top of the silverside means you are cutting along the grain or with the grain, which will help to keep the jerky tender.) Once you have cut one steak, you can then remove another from the freezer and cut that one. This quantity of marinade is good for about 650 g (1 lb 7 oz) of the thinly cut silverside; you can freeze the unused steaks for next time you make a batch of jerky. You should end up with lovely long strips of meat about 3 cm (1¼ inches) wide, 2–3 mm (1/16–1/8 inch) thick and of varying lengths.

In a glass bowl, combine all the remaining ingredients and mix well. Put the silverside strips into the marinade, mixing well, then cover with plastic wrap and refrigerate for 3 days. Give the meat a stir every day.

Preheat the oven to 80°C (175°F/Gas ¼), putting the oven fan on. (If your oven doesn't have a fan, you can leave the door slightly ajar to allow the air to circulate, but the cooking time might be longer this way.) Remove the meat from the bowl and lay the pieces flat on several layers of paper towel. Place more layers of paper towel on top and press firmly to soak up the excess marinade from the meat – the flavour is in the meat now, and you don't want the meat to be wet when you dry it in the oven as the meat may steam and become tough. Lay the meat strips out on wire racks, evenly spaced and not touching each other.

Place the racks in the oven and leave the door ajar so the air can circulate around the oven (this applies no matter whether your oven is conventional or fan-forced). It will take 3–3½ hours or so for the meat to dry, depending on how thick you actually ended up cutting it, what the air temperature is outside the oven and how your oven works. (I also like to turn the meat over once, about 2 hours into the drying process, as this helps to dry it evenly.) You don't want to dry the meat out so much that it crumbles into dust when you take a bite – the meat should be dry all the way through but pliable, and you should be able to tear it in half with your hands.

If you can stop yourself from eating all of this delicious jerky immediately, store the remainder in an airtight container with some paper towel in the bottom, or wrap it in some paper towel and put it in a zip-lock plastic bag. The jerky will be good for a couple of weeks – but I guarantee it will not last that long. This could well be the best beer accompaniment known to man!

MAKES 30–40 PIECES, DEPENDING ON HOW THICK YOU CUT THE SILVERSIDE

Belgian-style fried cheese croquettes

125 g (4½ oz/½ cup) unsalted butter
150 g (5½ oz/1 cup) plain (all-purpose) flour
420 ml (14½ fl oz/1⅔ cups) milk
125 g (4½ oz/1 cup) grated aged cheddar
    cheese; one with a bit of bite
140 g (5 oz/1 cup) chopped blue cheese
250 g (9 oz/2½ cups) grated gruyère cheese
3 free-range egg yolks
¼ teaspoon ground white pepper

¼ teaspoon ground nutmeg
¼ teaspoon chilli powder
¼ teaspoon paprika
olive oil, for deep-frying

FOR CRUMBING
150 g (5½ oz/1 cup) plain (all-purpose) flour
2 free-range eggs, beaten
100 g (3½ oz/1 cup) dry breadcrumbs

Line a 26 x 16 cm (10½ x 6¼ inch) flat-bottomed cake tin with plastic wrap, making sure there is plenty of wrap overhanging the sides.

Melt the butter in a frying pan over medium heat, then add the flour. Stirring constantly with a wooden spoon, cook for a few minutes to minimise the raw flour taste. Switch to a whisk and gradually whisk in the milk. Continue whisking as you bring the mixture to just below boiling, then reduce the heat and simmer for 5 minutes, stirring occasionally. The sauce should be thick and smooth, with the flour taste cooked out. Add the cheeses and allow to melt (but not boil). Remove from the heat.

Give the mixture a good stir to cool it a little, then add the egg yolks one at a time, mixing each one in thoroughly. Stir in the white pepper, nutmeg, chilli powder and paprika. Taste for seasoning and adjust – you may not need to add salt due to the saltiness of the blue cheese. Pour the mixture into the cake tin and smooth it down with a spatula. Fold the overhanging plastic wrap over the mixture, pressing it directly onto the surface. Refrigerate overnight.

Turn the chilled cheese mixture out onto a floured work surface. You can cut it into any shape you wish – triangles, squares, etc – or you can cut a portion and roll it out to form a long cylinder, then cut that into 3–4 cm (1¼–1½ inch) lengths. Coat these in the crumbing flour, dip them in the beaten egg, and finally coat well with the breadcrumbs. As you make them put them on a plate and then place in the freezer for about 10 minutes to set the crumbs.

Heat enough olive oil for deep-frying in a deep-sided frying pan over high heat. When the oil is very hot, fry the croquettes in batches until golden, about 5–8 minutes, depending on their size. Remove and drain on paper towels, then place in a warm oven while you cook the rest. Serve with toothpicks and a bowl of warmed chilli onion marmalade and some raspberry jam. The sweet–sour flavours from the marmalade and jam, mixed with hot, crunchy and creamy cheese, are perfect with a beer!

MAKES ABOUT 30

I love barbecued wings and couldn't decide which of my favourite spice recipes to include, so here are two of them! The sichuan mix is Asian-inspired, with a sweet-and-sour background, while the hot spice mix is more a Tex-Mex barbecue rub. Both of them are great for any occasion.

Oven-baked spicy chicken wings

8 free-range chicken wings
olive oil spray

SICHUAN SPICE MIX
4 teaspoons sichuan peppercorns
1½ teaspoons good-quality salt, such as
    Murray River or Maldon
1 teaspoon lemon pepper
½ teaspoon freshly ground black pepper
1 teaspoon garlic powder
¼ teaspoon ground cardamom
2 tablespoons rice flour

HOT SPICE MIX
½ teaspoon dried thyme
1 teaspoon good-quality salt, such
    as Murray River or Maldon
1 teaspoon garlic powder
½ teaspoon celery salt
1 teaspoon onion powder
1 teaspoon chilli powder
1½ teaspoons cayenne pepper
1 teaspoon ground cumin
1 teaspoon ground coriander
½ teaspoon mustard powder
2 tablespoons rice flour

Preheat the oven to 180°C (350°F/Gas 4). If using the sichuan spice mix, toast the sichuan peppercorns in a dry frying pan over medium–high heat until smoking. Transfer the peppercorns to a mortar and give them a good grinding with a pestle to break down the skins, then add the rest of the sichuan spice mix ingredients and grind together to form a well-combined powder. If using the hot spice mix, put all the spice mix ingredients in a mortar and grind together until you have a well-combined powder. (Grinding the powdered spices together breaks down the salt and gives a better mix.)

Put your spice mix in a clean plastic bag, then add the chicken wings and shake thoroughly so all the wings are well coated. Place the wings on a baking tray and lightly spray with olive oil. Bake for 40 minutes, or until they are cooked – if you poke the joint with a knife and the juices run clear, the wings are ready.

These wings are also great cooked on a barbecue via indirect medium–high heat (180°C/350°F) with the hood down; they will take about the same time as in the oven. If you barbecue the wings over direct heat, start with high heat for the first 15 minutes or so, turning the wings several times so they don't burn, then turn the heat to medium–low to finish the wings off for another 30–40 minutes. They'll be nicely charred and the juices will run clear if you poke the wing in the joint.
MAKES 8

When I make pizza at home, my kids always want me to make this pizza as a starter to get our tastebuds really going. As I get six pizzas out of the dough recipe below, I'll usually make two rosemary and garlic pizzas and then do the usual Italian-type toppings for the other four. If you only want to make a couple of pizzas you can freeze the remaining balls of risen dough to use another time. Or invite some friends around, buy some good handcrafted ales and have a pizza party!

Rosemary and garlic pizzas

PIZZA DOUGH

350 ml (12 fl oz) warm water
a good pinch of sugar
2 teaspoons olive oil
3 teaspoons dried yeast
600 g (1 lb 5 oz/4 cups) 'oo' flour or bread flour

TOPPING

8 garlic cloves, crushed
185 ml (6 fl oz/¾ cup) olive oil
6 tablespoons fresh rosemary leaves
6 teaspoons good-quality salt, such as Maldon
   or Murray River

Pour the water into a jug and add the sugar, olive oil and yeast. Give it a stir and let it sit for 10–15 minutes while the yeast gets going. It should develop a nice foamy head.

Put the flour in a large mixing bowl and mix ½ teaspoon salt through. Slowly add the yeast mixture to the flour and mix with a wooden spoon or your hand until you get a ball of dough – if you need to add a little more liquid, add some water to the jug that held the yeast mixture, swirl it around to pick up any leftover yeast, then add it to the dough. Turn the dough out onto a floured work surface and give it a good kneading for 10 minutes, or until you feel the consistency and texture change to a more smooth and silken feel.

Wipe or spray the inside of a large glass bowl with olive oil, then sprinkle flour around the inside so that it sticks to the oil – this stops the dough sticking to the bowl while it rises. Put the dough in the bowl and cover with plastic wrap. If your bowl is shallow, also spray and flour the undersurface of the plastic wrap where it might touch the dough as it rises. Put the dough in a warm place and let it rise until it doubles in size, about 1½–2 hours. (The time this actually takes depends on the weather and where you leave the bowl.)

While waiting for the dough to rise, combine the garlic and olive oil in a bowl and give it a stir to release the garlic's flavour into the oil.

Preheat the oven as hot as it will go. When the dough has doubled in size, tip it out onto a floured work surface, shape it into a log and cut into six equal portions. Roll each portion into a ball, dust with a little flour and cover with a tea towel (dish towel) until ready to use.

Use a pastry brush to brush your pizza trays with some of the garlic olive oil. Roll out a ball of dough to the size of a tray and place it on the tray. Brush the dough with the garlic olive oil, making sure you scoop up bits of the crushed garlic in the oil so they scatter around the pizza. Scatter 1 tablespoon of the rosemary over the top, then sprinkle with 1 teaspoon of the salt. Repeat with the remaining ingredients to make six pizzas.

Place in the oven and bake until cooked. How long this takes varies with your oven – in my oven it takes 8–10 minutes, on a pizza stone in the barbecue or a Weber kettle barbecue it takes 10–15 minutes, and in my Alfresco wood-fired pizza oven out the back it takes only about 90 seconds.

Sometimes I like to overcook this pizza as it makes it really crisp. Then, when I cut it, it breaks apart and is like having salty, garlic rosemary crisps!

MAKES 6 PIZZAS

Pork and duck rillettes

375 g (13 oz) pork belly
250 g (9 oz) pork neck
2 duck leg quarters
1 tablespoon sea salt
14 pepperberries or dried juniper berries
20 black peppercorns
6 cloves
4 dried bay leaves

4 garlic cloves, unpeeled
1 bouquet garni
2 tablespoons fresh lemon thyme
1 fresh rosemary sprig
330 ml (11¼ fl oz/1⅓ cups) of a good hoppy ale, such as Stone & Wood Pacific Ale, Wicked Elf Pale Ale or Arctic Fox American Pale Ale
200 g (7 oz) duck fat

Preheat the oven to 130°C (250°F/Gas 1). Take the skin off the pork belly, then cut the pork belly and the pork neck into 1 cm (½ inch) cubes. Cut the duck legs away from the thighs, remove the thigh bones, then cut the thigh meat the same size as the pork. Cut the duck meat away from the leg, then cut that into 1 cm (½ inch) cubes also. Put all the meat in a large baking dish and season with the sea salt. Place the pepperberries, peppercorns and cloves in a muslin (cheesecloth) bag, tie it up with kitchen string, then put the bag in the baking dish with the bay leaves, garlic cloves, bouquet garni, lemon thyme and rosemary. Pour the beer over and give the meat a really good mix to combine all the ingredients and evenly mix the salt through.

Bake for about 3 hours, turning the meat once every hour.

Once the meat is fall-apart tender, remove the dish from the oven and allow the meat to cool in the dish for 30 minutes so that it can 'rest' and soak up some of the cooking juices. Discard the bay leaves, the stalks from the rosemary and lemon thyme, the bouquet garni and the muslin bag, and remove the skins from the garlic cloves. Sit a colander in a large bowl and tip the meat into the colander. Allow the juices to drain into the bowl and leave the meat to cool. Once the meat is cool enough to handle, mash or shred it with your hands, a pair of forks or a potato masher until it is well shredded, mashing the roasted garlic cloves through. Return the meat to the bowl with the collected juices and mix well.

Melt the duck fat in a small saucepan over low heat and set aside to cool.

Distribute the meat evenly among six ramekins, pushing the meat down a little to set it with some firmness, then let it rest in the fridge to chill down for about 10 minutes. When cool, remove from the fridge and ladle some duck fat over each ramekin, covering the meat, then refrigerate once more. The duck fat will form a seal on top of the meat. The rillettes will keep in the fridge for several weeks, covered with plastic wrap.

Eat with crusty bread, a green salad, cornichons and walnuts.

SERVES 6

Marinated sardine fillets

8 sardine fillets

75 g (2½ oz/½ cup) plain (all-purpose) flour, seasoned with sea salt and freshly ground black pepper

2 tablespoons olive oil, approximately

½ brown onion, finely sliced

1 baby fennel bulb, trimmed and finely sliced (make sure you have the same amount of fennel as onion)

3 garlic cloves, finely sliced

a pinch of chilli flakes

1 tablespoon chopped fresh rosemary

1 tablespoon chopped fresh flat-leaf (Italian) parsley

125 ml (4 fl oz/½ cup) sherry vinegar

8 black peppercorns

4 dried bay leaves

toasted sourdough slices, to serve

Dredge the sardines in the seasoned flour and dust off the excess. Heat the olive oil in a frying pan over medium–high heat and fry the sardines until coloured and cooked through, about 3 minutes per side. Place the sardines in a shallow glass or ceramic dish that will fit them all in one layer.

Add a little more olive oil to the frying pan if needed and gently fry the onion, fennel, garlic and chilli flakes until softened, about 5 minutes. Add the rosemary, parsley, sherry, peppercorns, bay leaves and 60 ml (2 fl oz/¼ cup) water and bring to the boil. Turn down the heat and simmer until reduced by one-third. Pour the mixture over the sardines, cover the dish with plastic wrap and marinate for 12 hours – or up to 2 days – in the fridge.

Remove the dish from the fridge an hour or so before you plan to eat the sardines so they can come to room temperature. Simply serve a sardine fillet on a piece of toasted sourdough, with or without butter depending on your preference – but definitely with a cold beer!

SERVES 4 AS A SNACK

This is my basic salsa, to which you can add other ingredients – garlic, olives, beans, corn, anchovies and the like – to jazz it up and match it to other dishes. As it is, this is a great accompaniment to barbecued pork chops, chicken, turkey steaks, swordfish or anything else you may think of ... so when you make it, make extra. This salsa contains pickled jalapeños, which you can find in jars in the Mexican section in the supermarket; as far as I'm concerned they are a must-have item in the fridge. One tablespoon of chopped jalapeño will give a nice heat, 2 tablespoons will get you sweating!

Homemade salsa

2 large tomatoes (quite firm ones)
½ large avocado (not too soft; it needs to be firm enough to maintain its shape)
50 g (1¾ oz/⅓ cup) finely diced red onion
15 g (½ oz/¼ cup) chopped fresh coriander (cilantro)

1 tablespoon chopped pickled jalapeño chillies, or 2 tablespoons if you like it hot!
2 tablespoons lime juice
1 tablespoon olive oil
corn chips, to serve

We only want the flesh of the tomato and we want that flesh to be firm, so choose tomatoes that are quite firm. Cut a cross in the bottom of each tomato, put them in a bowl and cover with boiling water. Leave for a couple of minutes then, using tongs, remove one tomato and peel the skin away, starting from the cross you cut in the bottom. Put the tomato in a bowl of cold water, then peel the second tomato and place it in the cold water. (If you leave the tomatoes in the hot water too long they will start to cook and go soft and mushy. Putting them in the cold water stops the cooking process by zapping heat from them.)

Pat the tomatoes dry with paper towels. Cut them in half, then cut each half into thirds. Using a sharp knife or your fingers, cut or scrape away the seeds so that only the petal of flesh is left. (You can use the tomato seeds for a sauce, or put them in a salad.) Dry the excess moisture from the flesh with paper towels. Slice the segments thinly lengthways, then cut them across into small dice (you should have about 1 cup). Place in a glass bowl.

Dice the avocado the same size as the tomato and add to the bowl. Add the onion, coriander, jalapeño, lime juice and olive oil and give it all a really good but gentle mix. Taste, and if you feel the need, add a little salt, remembering that corn chips are also lightly salted. Serve straight away, with corn chips.

SERVES 4 AS A SNACK

Crisp fried garfish fillets

90 g (3 oz/½ cup) rice flour
¼ teaspoon ground cumin
¼ teaspoon smoked paprika
¼ teaspoon lemon pepper
¼ teaspoon sea salt
a pinch of freshly ground black pepper
10 whole garfish, filleted and boned
    (ask your fishmonger to do this)
olive oil, for pan-frying

CHILLI MAYO
1 teaspoon good-quality hot chilli paste
125 g (4½ oz/½ cup) good-quality mayonnaise

Put the flour and spices in a large bowl and mix thoroughly. Throw the garfish fillets into the seasoned flour and toss to coat them evenly. Dust off the excess flour.

Add enough olive oil to a frying pan or wok to shallow-fry the fish fillets. Heat the oil almost to smoking point and fry the fish in batches until golden and crisp. Remove from the pan using tongs or a slotted spoon and drain on paper towels. Keep warm in a low oven while you fry the remaining fish.

To make the chilli mayo, combine the chilli paste and mayonnaise in a small bowl and mix together until evenly combined.

Stack the fish on a plate, season to taste with extra sea salt and serve with the chilli mayo. Enjoy with a good cold beer.

SERVES 4

The simple dipping sauce with the oysters is all about the balance between sweet (palm sugar), salty (fish sauce), sour (lime juice) and heat (chilli). Everyone's tastebuds are different, so you may need to adjust the amounts slightly. The palm sugar adds a lovely delicate, full sweetness, but if you can't find it use caster (superfine) sugar. You can use any barbecue here, but it needs a hood or you won't be able to smoke anything in it. You'll also need a smoke box, which you can get at a barbecue shop, plus woodchips (I used a mix of hickory and Jack Daniel's-flavoured chips) and a cake rack.

Home-smoked oysters with Thai chilli dipping sauce

12 large oysters, fresh from the sea (while you're at it you may as well do two or three dozen!)
12 table crackers, to serve

CHILLI SAUCE
1½ teaspoons grated palm sugar (jaggery)
juice of 1 lime
1 bird's eye chilli, finely chopped
1½ teaspoons fish sauce

Put all the chilli sauce ingredients in a small bowl and give them a good stir. (I gently heat my sauce on the barbecue to make sure the palm sugar is melted and well integrated – you don't need to cook it, just make sure the sugar has dissolved completely.) Cover and set aside.

If using a Weber kettle barbecue you should have lit it 40 minutes ago! They are great to cook on, and especially great to smoke food on, but you need to think ahead in terms of getting them to the right temperature. Light the coals on only one side of the Weber as you don't need too much heat – say about 120°C (235°F) or so.

Shuck your oysters – you can't get them any fresher than that. Dunk the oyster meat into a pot of boiling water and let them boil for about 30 seconds to firm the flesh up a little. Scoop the oysters out and place on a clean, dry tea towel (dish towel), then pat completely dry. The oysters must be dry or the smoke will not stick to them.

Put the woodchips in the smoke box and place the box directly on top of the hot coals. Put the barbecue rack in, then place the cake rack on top of the barbecue rack on the other side of the Weber, away from the heat. Place the oysters on the cake rack and pull the barbecue hood down. Let the smoke do its thing for 25–35 minutes, turning the oysters after about 15 minutes. The oysters are done when they are firm to the touch, and not obviously raw or watery in the middle.

Tip the oysters into the bowl of chilli sauce and toss to coat. Serve each oyster on a table cracker.

SERVES 1, 2 OR 3, DEPENDING WHETHER YOU WANT TO SHARE THEM OR NOT!

Oven-baked chips

3 large potatoes (I can't go past Dutch cream)
olive oil, for drizzling
1–2 teaspoons chilli powder (optional)

1 tablespoon good-quality salt, such as Maldon
or Murray River pink salt

Preheat the oven to 190°C (375°F/Gas 5).

Peel, wash and dry the potatoes. Cut them in half down the middle lengthways, then cut each half in half again lengthways. Now cut three wedges out of each quarter. Throw all the chips into a large bowl, drizzle olive oil over them and sprinkle with the salt and the chilli powder, if using. Give the potatoes a really good toss so they are well coated.

Now here comes the bit that makes these chips really good: tip the pieces onto a baking tray and sit each one on its round back or rocker so that the flesh is facing up. This limits the contact of the potato to the baking tray, and thus stops the potato steaming and sticking to the tray. It also allows air and heat to circulate around more of the potato – kind of dry-roasting it, which means the chips will have a lovely dry and slightly crunchy skin, and won't be at all oily!

Bake for 35 minutes, or until the chips are browned and slightly crunchy on the outside, and soft and creamy in the middle. You don't have to turn them, just let them cook. I quite like to dip them in a chilli mayo – the one I use with the crisp fried garfish recipe on page 39.

Super simple, creamy, delicious and great with a beer!

SERVES 2

There is a very dangerous ingredient used in making pretzels the traditional German way, and that is caustic soda. The shaped pretzel dough is dipped in a lye bath – a diluted solution of caustic soda and water – for about 5 seconds. The pretzels are then baked in a hot oven, where a chemical reaction occurs that neutralises any dangers from the caustic and also creates that wonderful colour, texture and taste of the outside of the cooked pretzel. In my recipe I dip my formed pretzel dough into a boiling solution of bicarb soda and water, which achieves pretty much the same outcome as a lye bath without any of the inherent dangers of using caustic soda around the house. The purists will say that it is not as good as the traditional way – however I think it is, and as you are about to find out, these pretzels are pretty damn fine.

Pretzels

125 ml (4 fl oz/½ cup) milk
125 ml (4 fl oz/½ cup) hot water
2 teaspoons raw (demerara) or white sugar
2 teaspoons dried yeast
1 tablespoon butter, softened

300–450 g (10½ oz–1 lb/2–3 cups) plain
    (all-purpose) flour or bread flour
4 teaspoons bicarbonate of soda (baking soda)
good-quality salt flakes, such as Murray River
    or Maldon, for sprinkling

Combine the milk and hot water in a jug – the mixture should be warm but not hot. Add the sugar, yeast and butter and give it a stir, then set aside. After 5–10 minutes the yeast should be active and you will see lots of froth sitting on top.

Attach a dough hook to an electric mixer. Put 300 g (10½ oz/2 cups) of the flour into the mixing bowl and turn the mixer on. Give the yeast mixture a stir and then slowly add it to the flour, mixing all the time. The flour will come together but will still be quite wet, so add some of the remaining flour a handful at a time until the dough begins to form a ball. How much flour you need will depend on what type of flour you are using, as they take up liquid to different degrees. You don't want this dough to be too dry or stiff – it should be very soft and slightly sticky. Turn the dough out onto a lightly floured work surface and knead for 5 minutes or so, until the dough texture takes on a more silky character. Put the dough in a floured glass bowl – I usually spray some oil around the inside of the bowl and then sprinkle flour around it, as this stops the dough sticking to the glass. Cover with plastic wrap and set aside for an hour or two, or until the dough has at least doubled in size.

Preheat the oven to 230°C (450°F/Gas 8) and line two baking trays with baking paper. Once the dough has doubled in size, turn it out onto a floured work surface and shape it into a log. Cut this log in half, then cut each half into three pieces.

Roll each piece out to about 45 cm (18 inches) long – there is a trick to this, which is to leave a fatter bit in the middle. Imagine a snake has swallowed a football (or an oblong shape) which is sitting in the snake's middle. This fatter section should be about 6 cm ($2\frac{1}{2}$ inches) long. As this dough is quite soft you probably won't be able to roll it on the work surface, so the easiest way to roll it is to pick it up and hold it between your hands. With palms together and thumbs pointing to the roof, make like you are rubbing your hands together to warm them. Allow the dough to hang down, and as you rub your hands together the dough will slowly fall down, stretching out with the rolling action. This all makes perfect sense when you start doing it. Let the dough drop to the work surface and then repeat the process, starting from the other end. In order to get the fatter bit in the middle, start the rolling motion 4 cm ($1\frac{1}{2}$ inches) past the centre of the dough, and when you turn the dough and do the other side, start again 4 cm ($1\frac{1}{2}$ inches) past the middle section – and voila, you will end up with a 45 cm (18 inch) length of dough with a fat section in the middle. With practice comes perfection!

To make a pretzel shape, have a rolled 'snake' lying on the work surface in front of you. Pick up both ends and hold the dough above the work surface so it forms a big 'U' shape. Now cross your hands in a circular motion so that the 'U' swings, turns and twists around itself, then lay it flat on the work surface, still holding onto the ends. Place one end on top and to the side of the fat middle section, and the other end on the other side. Wet your finger (no, don't lick it – have a bowl with a little water nearby!) and dab where the two ends rest on the fat section to seal them down. Shape all the pretzels in the same way.

In a frying pan, bring 1 litre (35 fl oz/4 cups) water and the bicarbonate of soda to the boil. Dunk a pretzel in for about 10 seconds, then turn it over using tongs and let it sit for another 10 seconds. Remove from the boiling water with a slotted spoon and tongs and place on a prepared baking tray. Repeat with the other shaped pretzels, so you have three pretzels on each tray. Sprinkle generously with the salt flakes and bake for 10 minutes, or until the pretzels are a dark golden brown.

Remove from the oven and try to wait until they are a little cooler before you devour them. Of course, eat them with your favourite beer.

MAKES 6

Beer bites

Welcome to your world tour of cooking with beer. I hope this is the beginning of a long and wonderful culinary journey using beer as an ingredient. The following recipes give you a bit of a glimpse into the array of food styles that are possible when cooking with beer. Journey through Japan, Mexico, France, Australia, Asia, Spain and Italy, and when someone tells you that you can't use beer in a dish, make sure you prove them wrong! The rule is that if a dish has liquid in it then it may as well be beer – it's that simple. You can make these dishes as starters, upsize them to a main, or put them out as tapas. Whatever you do, serve them up with the beer you put in the dish and they – as well as you – will be winners.

Flathead are a beautiful eating fish with a sweet, delicate flavour and firm white flesh. They are pretty ugly to look at, though, as they have a large flat head, a big mouth and a couple of poisonous spikes. I get mine from my fishmonger, who is an expert at filleting. The 'tails' are in fact the fillets of the flathead – I don't know why they became known as flathead tails, but in the industry they are known as a 'V-cut flatty', which is the skinned and boned fillet.

I use olive oil for frying the flathead, but you could also use peanut or vegetable oil. I also don't really deep-fry but more shallow-fry the fish, which means you have to turn the fillets over when the first side is cooked.

This is a great beer batter because the rice flour gives a crisp, crunchy texture, and the saltiness and the spiciness from the sichuan peppercorns will make your mouth pop! To get a crisp result you want the batter to be as cold as possible, so make sure your beer has been in the freezer for at least 15 minutes before pouring it into the flour. You can even rest the batter in an ice bath while you make it.

Beer-battered sichuan flathead tails

2 tablespoons sichuan peppercorns
90 g (3¼ oz/½ cup) rice flour
1 tablespoon sea salt
¼ teaspoon ground white pepper

330 ml (11¼ fl oz) bottle of pilsner-style beer
olive oil, for shallow-frying
12 small flathead tails (100 g/3½ oz each), or
   6–8 large tails, cut in half into two long fillets

BEER NOTES
Try Peroni Nastro Azzurro, Trumer Pils or a good local craft-brewed pilsner such as Red Angus Pilsener or Blue Tongue Traditional Pilsner for this dish

Put the peppercorns in a small frying pan and dry-fry them gently until they smell fragrant and start to smoke. Grind to a powder using a mortar and pestle. Put the peppercorn powder in a bowl with the rice flour, salt and white pepper and give it all a good mix. Add about 125 ml (4 fl oz/½ cup) beer to the bowl and mix to a batter – I like a batter that's slightly thicker than pouring cream, but if you like your batter thin add more beer, or less if you like it even thicker. (Sip the rest while frying the fish!)

Heat about 2 cm (¾ inch) olive oil in a large saucepan or wok. You can tell the oil is at the right temperature when it begins to shimmer – you don't want it to reach smoking point as this will burn the fish. Drop the fish pieces into the batter and coat well. Carefully transfer the fish (I use my fingers for this, as tongs can tear the fish) to the hot oil and fry until golden, turning them over once. Depending on the size of your pot or wok, you would probably fry the fish in two batches. Remove from the oil using tongs or a slotted spoon and drain on paper towels.

Serve hot, with some lemon cheeks, tartare sauce or chilli mayo (see page 39).

SERVES 4

How thick or thin you like your batter is really a personal choice, and to some extent depends on your mood and what you are cooking. For instance if I was doing this dish with calamari, I would go for a lighter or thinner batter, but with prawns I prefer a heavier or thicker batter as the rice flour makes the batter really crunchy, and the prawns can carry that.

I use the Feral White ale here as it is a terrific wheat beer made with 50 per cent wheat malt, which adds a lovely smooth character to the beer. It is also made with an addition of coriander (cilantro) and orange peel, which gives the beer a fruity spiciness that really adds to the batter and the sweetness of the prawns.

Crisp beer-battered prawns

115 g (4 oz/⅔ cup) rice flour
100 g (3½ oz/⅔ cup) plain (all-purpose) flour
1 teaspoon sea salt
½ teaspoon freshly ground black pepper
½ teaspoon ground cumin

330 ml (11¼ fl oz) bottle of chilled Belgian-style wit ale, such as Feral White, Holgate White Ale or Hoegaarden Original White Ale
20 large raw prawns (shrimp), peeled and deveined, tails removed
750 ml (26 fl oz/3 cups) olive or peanut oil

Put the flours, salt, pepper and cumin in a large bowl and mix together until well combined. Pour in 250 ml (9 fl oz/1 cup) of the cold beer and mix into a batter using a whisk. When you are happy with the consistency of the batter (add a little more beer if you prefer a thinner batter), put all the prawns in and give them a good mix to coat.

Heat the oil in a wok over high heat. When it begins to smoke, carefully drop seven prawns into the oil and fry them, stirring gently so they don't stick together. After a couple of minutes, turn them over using tongs and continue to fry until cooked. (I turn them a few times so they cook evenly and don't get too brown.) Remove the prawns from the oil and drain on paper towels while you cook the remaining two batches.

Serve with chilli mayo (see page 39) or Thai chilli dipping sauce (see page 42), and a chilled glass of the beer you used in the batter.

SERVES 4

Witlof – sometimes spelled witloof and often called chicory or Belgian endive – is a lovely and unique bitter green vegetable. You will usually find it packaged in sets of two in the vegetable section of your supermarket or greengrocer. Occasionally red witlof is available, but there is really no difference in flavour.

Braised witlof with a beer and cheese sauce

20 g (¾ oz) unsalted butter
1 tablespoon plain (all-purpose) flour
125 ml (4 fl oz/½ cup) milk
125 ml (4 fl oz/½ cup) American-style pale ale

65 g (2½ oz/½ cup) grated gruyère cheese
sea salt and ground white pepper, for seasoning
8 small witlof (chicory/Belgian endive)
8 thick slices of ham, cut off the bone

To make the sauce, melt the butter in a saucepan over medium heat until it begins to foam, then gradually add the flour, stirring well as you add it. Let the mixture cook, stirring constantly, for a few minutes to cook out the flour taste – make sure you don't colour the roux by cooking it over too high a heat. Next, slowly whisk in the milk so that it combines well with the roux, then gradually whisk in the beer. If the sauce is too thick and you need to add more liquid, add equal amounts of beer and milk. You want the sauce to have a consistency a bit like thick pouring custard, and keep in mind that when you add the cheese the sauce will thicken a little more. When you're happy with the sauce consistency, add the cheese and mix it in until it melts. Add sea salt and ground white pepper to taste.

Place the witlof in a saucepan of gently simmering salted water and simmer for 5–10 minutes, or until cooked to your liking. You want it soft, but still with some bite or texture to it – make sure you don't overcook the witlof or it will become mushy and not very pleasant. Using a slotted spoon, remove the witlof from the pan and drain away any excess water. (If you want a little more flavour in the witlof, you could simmer it in a light chicken stock, or even a mixture of half water and half pale ale.)

Arrange two slices of ham on each plate, then place a hot witlof on top of each slice of ham. Spoon a generous amount of the sauce over the witlof.

Enjoy with a glass of the beer that you used in the sauce.

SERVES 4

BEER NOTES
Good pale ales for this dish include Epic Pale Ale from New Zealand, Hargreaves Hill Pale, Little Creatures Pale Ale or Three Sheets Pale Ale from the Lord Nelson Brewery Hotel

Porter is an ale made with dark and roasted malts that give the beer a dark ruby colour and flavours of coffee, chocolate, raisins and caramel, to name a few. It is a complex, full-flavoured ale that is perfect for this soup.

French onion and porter soup

45 g (1½ oz) unsalted butter
3 tablespoons olive oil
4 anchovy fillets
1 kg (2 lb 4 oz) brown onions, sliced
4 garlic cloves, chopped
1 tablespoon chopped fresh thyme
4 dried bay leaves
two 330 ml (11¼ fl oz) bottles of porter
    (I used James Squire Porter)

500 ml (17 fl oz/2 cups) beef stock
2 teaspoons brown sugar
1 teaspoon sea salt
1 teaspoon freshly ground black pepper
1 sourdough baguette
100 g (3½ oz/¾ cup) grated gruyère cheese

Put the butter and olive oil in a large saucepan over medium heat. Once the butter has melted and combined with the oil, add the anchovies and cook for 5 minutes, or until they have melted into the oil mixture.

Add the onion and stir well so that all the slices are well coated with the anchovy butter. Turn the heat down to medium–low and put a lid on the pan. Let the onion cook gently for 30 minutes, giving it a stir several times to make sure it cooks evenly. Add the garlic, stirring it through. Continue to cook gently, without the lid on, for another 30 minutes, stirring every 5 minutes or so to make sure the onion doesn't overcook or stick to the pan.

Add the thyme, bay leaves, beer, stock, sugar, salt and pepper, stirring well to combine all the flavours. Bring the soup to a simmer and cook for 30 minutes, allowing the liquid to reduce by one-third and the soup to thicken and darken in colour.

Preheat the grill (broiler) to high and line a baking tray with foil. Cut eight slices 1 cm (½ inch) thick on the diagonal from the baguette, then toast until golden. Place the toasts on the foil and cover each slice with a generous amount of cheese. Cook under the grill until the cheese has melted.

Ladle the soup into four bowls, then serve two gruyère toasts on top of each soup.

SERVES 4

German beer, cheese and sauerkraut soup

2 tablespoons olive oil

2 tablespoons unsalted butter, plus
    25 g (1 oz) extra

2 celery stalks, diced

1 onion, chopped

120 g (4 oz) speck, chopped

4–5 fresh thyme sprigs

1 tablespoon mustard powder

1 tablespoon worcestershire sauce

500 ml (17 fl oz/2 cups) German hefeweizen
    (wheat beer), such as Schofferhofer,
    Franziskaner or Erdinger

500 ml (17 fl oz/2 cups) good-quality chicken
    stock (make sure it's not too salty)

175 g (6 oz/1 cup) sauerkraut

125 ml (4 fl oz/½ cup) milk

125 ml (4 fl oz/½ cup) cream

125 g (4½ oz/1 cup) grated cheddar cheese

25 g (1 oz) plain (all-purpose) flour

Put the olive oil and butter in a deep saucepan over medium–high heat. When the mixture is hot, add the celery, onion and speck and cook, stirring, for about 5 minutes. Add the thyme, mustard powder, worcestershire sauce, beer and stock and bring to the boil, then reduce the heat and simmer for 15 minutes.

Add the sauerkraut and stir until the mixture comes back to a simmer, then stir in the milk and cream. Bring back to the boil and simmer for 5 minutes before adding the cheese, mixing the soup thoroughly to allow the cheese to melt evenly. Season to taste with sea salt and freshly ground black pepper.

Make a roux by melting the extra butter in a small saucepan over medium heat; when it foams, add the flour and stir well to combine. Continue to cook, stirring occasionally, to cook out the flour taste. When the roux begins to brown slightly, add a ladle of the soup to the pan and combine well using a whisk. Add a little more stock until you have a thin, runny paste. Mix this into the soup, a little at a time, stirring until the soup thickens. Serve hot.

SERVES 4–6

Jalapeño poppers in beer batter

150 g (5½ oz/1 cup) plain (all-purpose) flour
330 ml (11¼ fl oz) bottle of chilled American-style
    pale ale
16 fresh green jalapeño chillies, about 5–6 cm
    (2–2½ inches) long
250 g (9 oz/1 cup) cream cheese, softened

2–3 tablespoons finely chopped fresh chives,
    approximately
2–3 tablespoons finely chopped fresh mint,
    approximately
olive or peanut oil, for deep-frying

Make the batter first so it can stand and improve while you stuff the jalapeños. Put the flour in a bowl, season with sea salt, then whisk in the cold beer until you reach the consistency you prefer – you don't want it too thick or too thin. Keep the batter cold by resting it in the freezer while you prepare the jalapeños.

Place the jalapeños under a hot grill (broiler) and char the skins until black, turning the jalapeños so they blacken all over. Put them in a plastic bag to sweat for 5 minutes, then peel all the skin off, leaving the stems intact and long. Slice down one side and carefully remove the seeds and the membrane – these hold most of the heat, so if you want your jalapeños hot, leave some of the membrane and seeds in. However, I recommend you first make them without the seeds so you know what you are getting yourself into!

Put the cream cheese in a mixing bowl and add 2 tablespoons each of the chives and mint. Mix vigorously so that the herbs are thoroughly mixed through. It is quicker and easier to do this with electric beaters, otherwise prepare for a good workout with your wooden spoon and a bowl! Taste to check the flavour balance between the mint, chives and cheese and adjust if needed by adding a little more of one or both herbs. Using a teaspoon, carefully stuff each jalapeño with the cheese mixture until they are full and resemble their original shape before you chargrilled them. Carefully push the cut sides together over the cheese, so the jalapeño looks whole and intact.

Add enough oil to a wok, frying pan, saucepan or deep-fryer to deep-fry the jalapeños. Heat the oil to 180°C (350°F), or medium–high.

Remove the batter from the freezer. Holding the stuffed jalapeños by the stalks, carefully dip them in the batter, making sure they are well coated. Allow the excess to drip off, then gently lower them into the hot oil and cook for 3 minutes, or until golden. Depending on the size of your pan you may want to cook them in two or three batches. Remove from the oil using tongs or a slotted spoon and drain on paper towels.

Let them cool just a little, then enjoy with the beer you used for the batter.

SERVES 3–5, DEPENDING ON HOW GREEDY OR HUNGRY YOU ARE!

BEER NOTES
Try Arctic Fox
American Pale Ale,
Hargreaves Hill
Pale, Stone & Wood
Pacific Ale, Wicked
Elf Pale Ale or
Temple Pale Ale for
the batter

Caramelised scallops, crisp prosciutto and hollandaise de la beer

3 tablespoons white wine vinegar
60 ml (2 fl oz/¼ cup) pale ale, such as an
American-style pale ale or Arctic Fox American
    Pale Ale
ground white pepper, for seasoning
4 thin prosciutto slices
3 free-range egg yolks

200 g (7 oz) unsalted butter, melted
2 tablespoons olive oil
12 large scallops, white meat only
1 radicchio, either oval like a baby cos (romaine)
    lettuce, or round like a small iceberg lettuce,
    leaves separated

Preheat the oven to 200°C (400°F/Gas 6). In a small saucepan, bring the vinegar, beer and a pinch of ground white pepper to the boil. Cook until the liquid has reduced by two-thirds, then remove from the heat and allow to cool.

Place the prosciutto slices on a baking tray lined with baking paper and bake for 10 minutes, or until crisp. Remove from the oven and set aside. When cool enough to handle, cut or tear each slice into three long strips.

Fill a medium-sized saucepan one-quarter full of water. Bring to the boil, then turn the heat down so that the water is barely simmering – and when I say 'barely' I mean hardly simmering at all. On top of the saucepan place a heatproof glass bowl that fits snugly without coming into contact with the water. Put the egg yolks and the vinegar/beer reduction in the glass bowl and beat them together using a whisk. Continue to beat for 4 minutes or so – the mixture will double in size and thicken into a pale, foamy sauce. Continue to whisk as you gradually add the melted butter. Once all the butter has been added you should have a thick, creamy and buttery hollandaise sauce. Taste for seasoning and add a little sea salt if you want.

Put a non-stick frying pan over high heat and add the olive oil. Season the scallops generously with some sea salt, place in the pan and cook for 1–2 minutes, or until well coloured. Turn and cook the other side until caramelised, then remove from the pan and keep warm.

Put two or three radicchio leaves on each plate, then arrange three scallops on or around them. Spoon the hollandaise over or around the scallops, rest a crisp spear of prosciutto on each scallop and serve.

SERVES 4

I like blue cheese. There are some magnificent goat's and sheep's blues around, but if you find them too strong, just use a plain goat's cheese for these tarts, or even a good feta.

Onion, stout and goat's cheese tarts

3 tablespoons olive oil
2 brown onions, sliced
1 red onion, sliced
150 g (5½ oz) fennel bulb, sliced
3 garlic cloves, finely sliced
180 g (6 oz) Swiss brown mushrooms, sliced
2 teaspoons raw (demerara) sugar
125 ml (4 fl oz/½ cup) stout
2 teaspoons fresh thyme leaves

2 sheets frozen puff pastry, thawed
120 g (4¼ oz) blue goat's cheese, such as
    Red Hill Mountain Goat Blue
1 free-range egg, beaten

ROCKET SALAD
125 g (4½ oz) rocket (arugula)
2 tablespoons olive oil
2 tablespoons balsamic vinegar

Heat half the olive oil in a frying pan over medium–high heat. Add all the onion and stir-fry for a few minutes so it is well coated with the oil. Reduce the heat to low and cook for 30 minutes, stirring often. Remove the onion from the pan and keep warm.

Turn the heat up to medium, add the remaining olive oil and gently fry the fennel for about 5 minutes. Add the garlic and cook gently for 10 minutes. Add the mushrooms and cook for 5 minutes, then add the sugar, stout and thyme and cook for another 5 minutes. Stir the onion back in, season well with sea salt and freshly ground black pepper and continue to cook until most of the liquid has evaporated, 5–10 minutes. Remove from the heat and allow to cool.

Preheat the oven to 200°C (400°F/Gas 6) and line two baking trays with baking paper. Lay the pastry sheets on a lightly floured work surface. (There's nothing wrong with using ready-made puff pastry; nothing wrong with making your own either!) Cut away a strip 7 cm (2¾ inches) long from one side of each sheet – you will now have two rectangular shapes. Place on the baking trays. With a sharp knife, score an inside rectangle about 2 cm (¾ inch) in from the edge of the pastry, forming a border.

Divide the onion mixture evenly between the two pastry sheets, making sure it stays inside the scored area, leaving the border clean. Crumble the cheese over the onion mixture. Brush the borders with the beaten egg and bake for 12–15 minutes, or until the borders have risen and are a dark golden brown.

Meanwhile, put the rocket in a bowl and drizzle with the olive oil and balsamic vinegar. Add a sprinkle of salt and toss well to combine.

Cut each tart in half and enjoy with the rocket salad and a glass of stout.

SERVES 4

BEER NOTES
For this dish try a Coopers Best Extra Stout, or Mountain Goat Surefoot Stout – a lovely full-bodied and bitter stout

This is a great breakfast or lunch dish, and also makes a great late-night snack. Just prepare it the day before and have it in the fridge ready to go whenever you feel like it!

One-pot three-bean eggs

75 g (2½ oz/⅓ cup) dried black-eyed peas
75 g (2½ oz/⅓ cup) dried red kidney beans
75 g (2½ oz/⅓ cup) dried borlotti (cranberry) beans
45 ml (1½ fl oz) olive oil
1 onion, chopped
2 garlic cloves, chopped
1 small red chilli, finely chopped
½ red capsicum (pepper), cut into long strips
2 tablespoons tomato paste (concentrated purée)

440 g (15½ oz) tin chopped tomatoes
1 tablespoon worcestershire sauce
1 tablespoon brown sugar
330 ml (11¼ fl oz) bottle of stout (I used Red Hill Brewery Imperial Stout)
250 g (9 oz) smoked pork shoulder or kassler, cut into small chunks
25 g (1 oz/½ cup) fresh basil leaves
1 teaspoon fresh marjoram
8 free-range eggs

Soak the dried beans in a large bowl of cold water overnight. Or, take this shortcut: put them in a large glass microwave dish, add 1 litre (35 fl oz/4 cups) water, place in the microwave with a lid on and cook on high for 11 minutes. Remove from the microwave and set the bowl aside with the lid still on until you need the beans.

Heat the olive oil in a large saucepan over medium–high heat, then add the onion. Stir well to coat with the oil, then turn the heat down and sweat the onion for about 8 minutes. Add the garlic, chilli and capsicum and cook over medium heat for another 8 minutes, stirring occasionally. Stir in the tomato paste and cook for several minutes, then add the tomatoes and cook for several minutes more.

Add the worcestershire sauce, sugar, beer and pork and stir while the mixture comes to the boil. Add half the basil, the marjoram and 250 ml (9 fl oz/1 cup) water and give it all a good mix. Season with sea salt and freshly ground black pepper.

Drain the beans and add them to the pan. Mix well, put the lid on and simmer gently for a couple of hours, or until the beans are tender. Check and stir occasionally, adding a little more basil each time. Allow to cool before storing in an airtight container in the fridge for up to a week, or portion the mixture out and freeze until needed.

When you're ready for your one-pot three-bean eggs, preheat the oven to 230°C (450°F/Gas 8). Take the bean mixture out of the fridge and heat enough of it in your microwave to fill eight ovenproof ramekins about three-quarters full. Put the hot beans into the ramekins and make a little well in the centre. Crack an egg into each well, then bake for 10–15 minutes, or until the egg is set.

MAKES 8

BEER NOTES
You could also use Coopers Best Extra Stout, or even a dark ale such as a porter, a Guinness, or even a dark lager such as a Matilda Bay Dogbolter

On the Stove

Cooking on the stovetop in a frying pan has a lot in common with painting a picture. You take all these separate elements and put them together in a certain order and at the end, when you plate up, you have a complete story. A frying pan is like an artist's palette, where colours and flavours are mixed and combined to create something greater than the original components. Imagine creamy white leek, fiery red chilli, buttery crushed garlic, green, red and yellow capsicums (peppers), rich muddy-red chorizo, pink pork fillets, purple and white onion, copper saffron threads, shiny purple-skinned eggplants (aubergines), ruddy brown paprika, ruby-red ale, pearly white rice, green and black olives, vibrant yellow lemon, green herbs and there it is – your masterpiece gently simmering away on the stove awaiting to nourish, delight and excite all the senses.

A good friend of mine is the brewer for True South in the Melbourne suburb of Black Rock. I was a bit cheeky one day as I went in to see her with a large jar and begged her to give me some of her dark ale out of the fermenter. She did and this is the beer I used for this recipe. It has some coffee and chocolate overtones, is very malty and has a very smooth hop character – perfect for a lamb tagine.

Dark ale lamb tagine

MARINATED LAMB

1 kg (2 lb 4 oz) leg of lamb, boned and cut into
    4 cm (1½ inch) chunks
1 teaspoon ground cumin
1 teaspoon garlic powder
1 teaspoon ground coriander
1 teaspoon cayenne pepper
½ teaspoon ground turmeric
½ teaspoon celery salt
½ teaspoon ground cloves
½ teaspoon ground cinnamon
½ teaspoon ground cardamom
500 ml (17 fl oz/2 cups) True South Dark Ale

2 tablespoons olive oil
1 onion, halved and sliced
2 garlic cloves, sliced
½ teaspoon dried thyme
2 lemon peel strips, white pith removed
250 ml (9 fl oz/1 cup) good-quality beef stock
3 carrots, cut into batons
220 g (8 oz/1 cup) pitted prunes
310 g (11 oz/2 cups) frozen peas
chopped fresh coriander (cilantro), to garnish

Put the lamb in a large bowl. Add all the marinade spices and season with sea salt and freshly ground black pepper. Give the lamb a good toss so that the chunks are all covered by the spices, then pour the ale over and give it a stir. Cover with plastic wrap and marinate in the fridge for 24 hours, stirring every now and then.

Bring the lamb to room temperature. Put a tagine or flameproof casserole dish over medium–high heat and add the olive oil. When the oil is hot, add the onion and sweat for 5 minutes, or until translucent. Add the garlic and cook, stirring, for another 5 minutes.

Remove the lamb pieces from the marinade and shake off the excess marinade, reserving 250 ml (9 fl oz/1 cup). Add the lamb to the tagine and brown over high heat, stirring and turning often so it cooks evenly. Add the thyme and lemon peel and cook for a few minutes more. Pour in the stock and reserved marinade, bring to the boil, then turn the heat down to a gentle simmer. Put the lid on and cook for 45 minutes.

Mix the carrot and prunes through the liquid. Cook, covered, for 45 minutes – the meat should now be very tender. Add the peas and cook for another 10 minutes.

Garnish with the coriander and serve with couscous.

SERVES 4

BEER NOTES
If you can't get True South Dark Ale you could use a porter such as Lord Nelson Old Admiral, James Squire Porter or White Rabbit Dark Ale

Chicken and leek pie

3 tablespoons olive oil
2 free-range chicken breasts (about 600 g/
　　1 lb 5 oz), cut into small cubes
a pinch of dried thyme
a pinch of ground cumin
1 leek, white part only, quartered lengthways,
　　then finely sliced
1 garlic clove, crushed
2 carrots, diced
2 celery stalks, diced
3 potatoes, peeled and diced

115 g (4 oz/¾ cup) frozen peas
3 sheets frozen puff pastry, thawed
1 free-range egg, beaten
sesame seeds, for sprinkling

VELOUTÉ SAUCE
30 g (1 oz) unsalted butter
30 g (1 oz) plain (all-purpose) flour
250 ml (9 fl oz/1 cup) good-quality chicken
　　stock, heated
250 ml (9 fl oz/1 cup) saison ale

Preheat the oven to 200°C (400°F/Gas 6). Lightly grease six individual 250 ml (9 fl oz/ 1 cup) capacity pie dishes.

Heat half the olive oil in a large frying pan over medium–high heat. Add the chicken and cook, stirring, until the meat is sealed and has turned white. (You don't want to cook the chicken all the way through at this point, as it will finish cooking in the pie.) Stir the thyme, cumin and some sea salt and freshly ground black pepper through the chicken until well distributed, then transfer the mixture to a bowl.

Add the remaining oil to the pan and fry the leek over medium heat for a few minutes. Reduce the heat, add the garlic and fry gently for a few minutes more. Add the carrot, celery and potato and cook for a few minutes, stirring to stop the vegetables sticking on the base of the pan. Allow the vegetables to cook gently over low heat while you make the velouté sauce.

Melt the butter in a saucepan over medium–low heat, then stir in the flour to make a roux. Cook gently for a few minutes to cook out the flour taste, then slowly pour in the stock and then the beer, mixing until you have a smooth, thick sauce. Season with sea salt and freshly ground black pepper and stir in any juices from the chicken.

Add the sauce to the vegetables and simmer until the vegetables are just tender, 25–30 minutes. Add the peas and chicken and simmer for 5 minutes to warm through.

Before filling the pie dishes, place two of them upside down on a sheet of puff pastry, then cut around them about 1 cm (½ inch) out from the dish. Repeat with the other two pastry sheets to give six pie lids. Spoon the mixture into the pie dishes. Brush beaten egg around the outer rims of the dishes and fit each with a puff pastry lid, pressing the outer edges to the egg to seal. Brush the top of the pies with beaten egg, then cut a cross in their centre so steam can escape. Sprinkle with sesame seeds and bake for 10 minutes, or until the pastry has risen and is golden brown and crisp.

MAKES 6

BEER NOTES
You could use a saison from Aussie micro-breweries Temple Brewing Company, Bridge Road Brewers or Otway Estate, or try the famous Belgian ale Saison Dupont

Chimay is one of only seven Trappist breweries in the world, where the beer is made in a Trappist monastery by Trappist monks. The Trappist monks from Chimay in Belgium have been making their beers since 1862 and have focused on three main beers – Chimay White or Cinq Cents (8 per cent), Chimay Red (7 per cent) and Chimay Blue (9 per cent). I love them all as they are big, malty, musty, yeasty beers with lots of character and alcohol. There is nothing better than sipping on a Chimay at the end of an evening, either with some cheese and dried muscatels, or just on its own. Chimay Blue is one of my all-time favourite beers and will work brilliantly in this dish, as does the Red; the White, however, tends to be a little bitter when you cook with it, so I normally don't.

Any of the Trappist beers would work here, so give them a go and see what difference each beer makes. The other Trappist breweries are Orval, Westmalle, Rochefort, Westvleteren, Koningshoeven and Achel.

Beef beer bourguignon

90 ml (3 fl oz) olive oil, approximately
1 leek, white part only, finely chopped
2 celery stalks, diced
100 g (3½ oz) piece of hot pancetta, diced
1 kg (2 lb 4 oz) stewing beef, cut into 4 cm (1½ inch) chunks
1 bunch (20 g/¾ oz) fresh lemon thyme
9 baby onions, peeled
7 garlic cloves
3 tablespoons Madeira
1 tablespoon plain (all-purpose) flour
3 carrots, sliced on the diagonal 1 cm (½ inch) thick

two 330 ml (11¼ fl oz) bottles of a Trappist ale, such as Chimay Red or Chimay Blue
250 ml (9 fl oz/1 cup) good-quality beef stock
3 orange peel strips, white pith removed
3 dried bay leaves
125 g (4½ oz/½ cup) tinned crushed tomatoes
8 Swiss brown mushrooms, wiped clean and quartered
300 g (10½ oz) green beans, topped, tailed and cut into 5 cm (2 inch) lengths
3 tablespoons chopped fresh flat-leaf (Italian) parsley

Heat half the olive oil in a deep flameproof casserole dish over medium heat. Add the leek and cook, stirring, for about 5 minutes. Add the celery and pancetta and cook for another 5 minutes, then remove the mixture from the dish.

Add another 2 tablespoons of the olive oil to the dish and brown half the beef over high heat until well coloured. Shake the bunch of thyme over the beef while it browns so that a good pinch of leaves falls on top. When the beef is browned, remove it from the dish using tongs and place on a plate lined with paper towels to soak up any excess oil. Brown the rest of the beef, again adding some thyme, then remove to the plate with the other beef.

Return the dish to medium–high heat, add a little more oil if needed, then add the onions and garlic. Stir them around the dish and cook for about 5 minutes, or until the onions are coloured and their fragrance fills the air. Add the Madeira and scrape the base of the dish with a wooden spoon to deglaze and loosen all the stuck-on bits. Tip the beef back in and scatter the flour over. Give it all a good mix, then add the carrots and the leek, celery and pancetta mixture and stir the ingredients through.

Still over medium–high heat, add the beer and stock and stir until the mixture comes to the boil. Add the orange zest, bay leaves, tomatoes, a good pinch of sea salt and some freshly ground black pepper. Stir again, then reduce the heat to a simmer. Cover with a lid and simmer for about 40 minutes.

Add the mushrooms and cook, with the lid off, for 20 minutes. Add the beans and cook for a final 10 minutes. Remove from the heat and stir the parsley through.

Serve with creamy mashed potato or some boiled baby potatoes.

SERVES 4

Hoegaarden seafood risotto

2 litres (70 fl oz/8 cups) good-quality
    chicken stock
50 g (1¾ oz) unsalted butter
1 onion, finely diced
100 g (3¼ oz) speck, finely diced
3 tablespoons chopped fresh coriander (cilantro)
300 g (10½ oz/1⅓ cups) arborio rice
330 ml (11¼ fl oz) bottle of Belgian-style
    wheat beer

16 raw prawns (shrimp), peeled and deveined
140 g (5 oz/1 cup) frozen peas
12 scallops; if the roes are still attached, separate
    these from the scallop meat and reserve
200 g (7 oz) baby calamari or squid tubes,
    cleaned, scored in a diamond pattern,
    then cut into 1 x 3 cm (½ x 1¼ inch) strips

Pour the stock into a saucepan and bring to the boil. Turn the heat down and maintain a gentle simmer.

Melt the butter in a large heavy-based saucepan over medium–high heat. When foaming, add the onion and cook until translucent. Add the speck and fry, stirring, until browned, being careful not to brown the onion. Add 1 tablespoon of the coriander for flavour, then add the rice. Stir well to coat the rice with the buttery mixture and cook for 3 minutes. Add the beer and stir thoroughly.

Let the rice absorb the beer before adding the first ladleful of simmering stock. Stir it into the rice, and when it is all absorbed, add another ladleful. Check the heat: the rice should not absorb the stock too quickly or slowly – it should take about half an hour for all of the stock to be absorbed. When you are down to the last two ladlefuls of stock, test the rice for texture. It should be soft on the outside, but have a slight bite in the middle, similar to pasta when it is cooked al dente.

When you think you are getting close to this stage, add the prawns and peas and allow them to cook for a couple of minutes. Add some more hot stock, then add the scallops, the roes (if your scallops had them) and the calamari, stirring well so they are covered by the rice. Cook for a few minutes, then add the last ladleful of stock and the remaining coriander. Cook, stirring, until most of this liquid has been absorbed and the seafood is cooked. The rice should have a glossy, smooth and creamy texture. Taste and season with sea salt and freshly ground black pepper as needed.

Depending on how long the rice takes to cook, you may not need to use all the stock, or you may need extra. Keep on tasting as you cook, testing for how the rice is absorbing the stock and whether or not you want to add more herbs or seasoning. You can also use the prawns unshelled for more flavour, but I find it too messy to eat them that way.

Serve with a simple green salad.

SERVES 4

BEER NOTES
Wheat beers you could use for this recipe include Hoegaarden Witbier, Feral White, Wicked Elf Witbier or Bright Brewery Razor Witbier

Cockle and beer butter pasta

1 tablespoon unsalted butter, plus 50 g (1¾ oz)
    extra, chopped
1 tablespoon olive oil
1–2 small red chillies, or to taste, finely chopped
2 garlic cloves, finely chopped
3 small spring onions (scallions), white part only,
    finely chopped
3 tablespoons chopped fresh coriander (cilantro)

200 ml (7 fl oz) good-quality chicken stock
200 ml (7 fl oz) German or Belgian-style
    wheat beer
1 bunch (200 g/7 oz) broccolini, cut into 3 cm
    (1¼ inch) lengths
650 g (1 lb 7 oz) cockles
400 g (14 oz) angel hair pasta
lemon wedges, to squeeze over the pasta

Fill a large saucepan with water, add a generous pinch of salt and bring to the boil over high heat.

Meanwhile, heat the 1 tablespoon butter and the olive oil in a large frying pan over medium–high heat. When the butter begins to foam, add the chilli, garlic and spring onion. Fry for a minute or two, then reduce the heat to medium and allow the mixture to cook for 2–3 minutes more, being careful not to burn it. Add the coriander and cook for another 2 minutes or so. Turn the heat up to high and add the stock and beer. When the liquid boils, reduce the heat so the liquid is at a rolling simmer. Continue simmering until the liquid is reduced by two-thirds.

Once reduced, add the broccolini. Give the mixture a good stir, season with sea salt and freshly ground black pepper, then add the cockles, stirring them through the sauce. Put the lid on and cook for 3 minutes, giving the pan a good shake once or twice during this time.

Cook the pasta in the boiling water until al dente – this pasta only takes about 2 minutes to cook. Drain the pasta and add to the frying pan along with the extra chopped butter and a squeeze of lemon juice. Give it all a good mix around so the butter melts and the pasta is well coated with the sauce.

Divide among four bowls and serve at once, with wedges of lemon on the side.

SERVES 4

BEER NOTES
Try Redback
Original, Red Hill
Brewery Wheat
Beer, Tuatara Hefe
from New Zealand,
2 Brothers Trickster,
Feral White or
Wicked Elf Witbier

Stout and preserved lemon risotto

15 g (½ oz) dried porcini mushrooms
2 litres (8 cups) good-quality chicken stock, approximately; homemade is best
3 tablespoons butter
1 onion, finely diced
300 g (10½ oz/1⅓ cups) arborio rice

250 ml (9 fl oz/1 cup) Coopers Best Extra Stout or Mountain Goat Surefoot Stout
¼ of a preserved lemon, salty flesh discarded, the rind finely chopped
310 g (11 oz/2 cups) frozen peas
2 tablespoons grated parmesan cheese

Soak the mushrooms in enough boiling water to cover for 10 minutes. Squeeze the mushrooms dry, reserving 60 ml (2 fl oz/¼ cup) of the liquid. Chop the mushrooms finely and set aside.

Meanwhile, put the stock in a saucepan over high heat and bring to the boil, then turn the heat down and keep the stock at a simmer.

Melt 2 tablespoons of the butter in a large saucepan over medium–low heat. Add the onion and sweat it down, stirring often, until softened. Add the rice and stir to coat it thoroughly, then cook for about 1 minute. Throw in the mushrooms and the reserved soaking liquid, then stir through the rice.

Once the liquid from the mushrooms has been absorbed by the rice, add the beer. Stir the rice constantly until the beer has been absorbed, then add a ladleful of the simmering stock and stir while it is being absorbed. Repeat this process until you have about one and a half ladlefuls of stock left.

Add the preserved lemon and peas, then the last of the stock. Stir to combine, and when most but not all of the liquid has been absorbed, turn off the heat. Add the remaining butter and the parmesan and mix through well – you should now have a rich, creamy, smooth and fragrant risotto. Season to taste with sea salt and freshly ground black pepper.

If you wish you can serve the risotto with a simple mixed lettuce salad containing rocket (arugula), dressed simply with olive oil and balsamic vinegar. The risotto is also a great accompaniment to barbecued quail or spatchcock (poussin).

SERVES 4

BEER NOTES
An imperial stout such as Red Hill Imperial Stout would also be great for this recipe as it is strong in flavour, bitterness and alcohol

Chilli con carne

3 tablespoons olive oil
1 onion, diced
2 carrots, diced
2 celery stalks, diced
1 chorizo sausage, diced
2 garlic cloves, chopped
1 small red chilli, sliced
3 teaspoons ground cumin
3 teaspoons ground coriander
3 teaspoons smoked paprika
1½ teaspoons ground oregano
1½ teaspoons Mexican chilli powder (available from large supermarkets and grocery stores)
350 g (12 oz) minced (ground) pork
350 g (12 oz) minced (ground) beef

2 tablespoons pickled jalapeño chillies, chopped, plus 1 tablespoon of the jalapeño pickling liquid
1 banana chilli, sliced
330 ml (11¼ fl oz) bottle of weissbock, such as Red Hill Brewery Weizenbock
440 g (15½ oz) tin chopped tomatoes
440 g (15½ oz) tin red kidney beans, rinsed and drained
125 g (4½ oz) green beans, topped and tailed, then cut into 1 cm (½ inch) lengths
1 large zucchini (courgette), diced
1 fresh jalapeño chilli, seeded and sliced
3 tablespoons chopped fresh coriander (cilantro), plus extra, to garnish

Heat the olive oil in a large saucepan over medium heat. Add the onion, carrot and celery and cook, stirring, for about 8 minutes, or until the onion is translucent. Add the chorizo and cook for another 5 minutes. Now add the garlic and chilli and cook, stirring, for 3 minutes or so. Add the spices and oregano and stir for several minutes, until the mixture is lovely and fragrant.

Turn up the heat, add the pork and beef and cook until browned, using a wooden spoon to break up any lumps, and stirring to combine all the ingredients and flavours.

Stir in the pickled jalapeño, pickling liquid, banana chilli, beer, tomatoes and kidney beans. Bring to the boil, then turn down the heat and allow to simmer gently for 20–25 minutes, stirring every now and then.

Add the green beans, zucchini and fresh jalapeño and simmer for 15 minutes. Taste for seasoning and add sea salt and freshly ground black pepper as required. Chilli con carne should be thick and rich but not dry, so stir in a little water or beer to loosen it if you need to. Conversely it should not be too wet or soupy, which is why I cook it without a lid.

Just before serving, stir the coriander through. Serve in bowls over a mixture of basmati and jasmine rice, garnished with the extra chopped coriander.

SERVES 6

BEER NOTES
Weissbock is a strong, usually dark, 7–9% German-style wheat beer. It has some toasty, chocolatey notes, along with the typical clove and banana ester characters you expect in a German wheat beer

Crumbed sardines with sou' western pasta

100 g (3½ oz/½ cup) dried black-eyed peas
200 g (7 oz) angel hair pasta or spaghettini
3 tablespoons lime juice
60 ml (2 fl oz/¼ cup) Belgian-style wit beer
1 tablespoon butter
½ red onion, finely diced
½ long red chilli, seeded and very finely diced
25 g (1 oz/½ cup) chopped fresh coriander
    (cilantro)
1 large tomato, peeled, seeded and finely diced

CRUMBED SARDINES
100 g (3½ oz/1 cup) dry breadcrumbs
25 g (1 oz/¼ cup) grated parmesan cheese
1 free-range egg
150 g (5½ oz/1 cup) plain (all-purpose) flour
6 butterflied sardine fillets
olive oil, for shallow-frying

Soak the black-eyed peas overnight in plenty of cold water. Drain them, place in a saucepan, cover with cold water – do not salt the water! – and bring to the boil. Turn the heat down to a rolling simmer and cook for about 35 minutes, or until tender. Drain the peas, reserving about 185 ml (6 fl oz/¾ cup) of the cooking liquid for the sauce.

If you forget to soak the peas overnight, here's a quick method. Put them in a glass microwave bowl and cover with about 750 ml (26 fl oz/3 cups) water. Cover with a lid and microwave on high for about 11 minutes.

To crumb the sardines, combine the breadcrumbs and parmesan and spread out on a plate. Beat the egg in a bowl and set aside. Put the flour in a clean plastic bag and season with sea salt and freshly ground black pepper. Add the sardine fillets and gently shake the bag to coat the sardines with the flour. Remove the sardines from the bag, shaking off the excess flour. Dip them into the beaten egg, making sure they are completely covered, then dredge them in the breadcrumb mixture, pressing the sardines into the mixture to coat them well.

Heat enough olive oil for shallow-frying (about 1 cm/½ inch) in a frying pan over medium–high heat. Fry three sardines at a time, turning them often so they cook evenly without burning. When golden brown, remove from the oil using tongs and place on paper towels to drain. Place in a warm oven while the next batch is cooking.

Meanwhile, fill a large saucepan with water, add a generous pinch of salt and bring to the boil over high heat. Add the pasta and cook until just al dente.

Put the lime juice and beer in a frying pan over medium–high heat and bring to the boil. Add the butter and stir until melted. Stir in the onion and chilli, then add the coriander, black-eyed peas and lastly the tomato. You don't want to cook the onion or tomato, just warm them through. If you can, time all this so that the pasta is ready to put into the frying pan just after you have added the tomato.

Using tongs, take the pasta out of the boiling water and put it straight into the pan with the sauce. It is okay to not drain the pasta, as the extra water clinging to it will add volume and flavour to the sauce. Mix thoroughly.

Stack three sardines on top of each other on one side of a plate. Using a fork, twirl half the pasta and place it next to the sardines, carefully removing the fork so that the pasta stands up in a twirled tower. Repeat on another plate with the remaining sardines and pasta. Spoon the sauce remaining in the pan over the pasta towers and around the plates.

Serve with a side salad.

SERVES 2

BEER NOTES
Suitable wit beers for this dish include Hoegaarden Witbier, Feral White, Wicked Elf Witbier and Holgate White Ale

Fish pie

POACHED FISH

125–150 g (4½–5½ oz) fillet of white-fleshed
    fish (such as ling, perch, blue eye cod,
    flathead), skin off
1 large ocean trout fillet, skin on
185 ml (6 fl oz/¾ cup) milk
185 ml (6 fl oz/¾ cup) La Chouffe or saison ale
2 tablespoons finely chopped fresh tarragon

2 tablespoons olive oil
½ leek, white part only, finely diced
1 carrot, finely diced
1 celery stalk, finely diced

6 raw prawns (shrimp), peeled and deveined,
    tails left on
8 scallops, with roe
25 g (1 oz) unsalted butter
25 g (1 oz) plain (all-purpose) flour
1 teaspoon dijon mustard
a squeeze of lemon juice
40 g (1½ oz/⅓ cup) grated cheddar cheese,
    or for extra character use a smoked cheese
a pinch of ground white pepper
3 potatoes, peeled and each cut into eight pieces
milk, cream and extra unsalted butter, for making
    mashed potatoes

Preheat the oven to 180°C (350°F/Gas 4).

Firstly, poach the fish. Place all the fish fillets in an ovenproof rectangular dish and pour the milk and beer over them. Season with sea salt and freshly ground black pepper, then scatter the tarragon over the top. Cover tightly with foil and bake for 8–10 minutes, or until the fish is soft and flaking. Remove the fish, reserving the poaching liquid. Remove and discard the skin from the ocean trout. (I leave it on for the poaching process as it adds extra flavour to the poaching liquid.) Break the fish into large flakes, set aside in a covered bowl and keep warm. Increase the oven temperature to 220°C (425°F/Gas 7).

Heat the olive oil in a frying pan over medium heat and fry the leek, carrot and celery for about 10 minutes, until softened and slightly coloured. Stir in the prawns and scallops, then continue to fry until the prawns and scallops are just cooked. Remove from the heat.

Melt the butter in a saucepan over medium heat. Once it is foaming, add the flour and stir to combine. Continue to cook for 2–3 minutes, stirring to cook the flour taste out of the roux. Add the reserved poaching liquid a little at a time, whisking until it is well combined and the sauce begins to thicken. Add the mustard and continue to stir over the heat until the sauce thickens. Add the lemon juice and cheese and stir until the cheese is well melted. Season with the white pepper and taste to see if you need to season with salt (the cheese will have added some saltiness to the sauce). Remove from the heat.

Bring the potato pieces to the boil in a saucepan of salted water. Cook until tender, then drain. Mash the potato over gentle heat, adding a little milk, cream and extra butter until you have the texture you require – you want the mash to be creamy, buttery and slightly firm.

Put the poached fish in a deep ovenproof pie dish with the prawns, scallops and vegetables and give it a bit of a mix. (Alternatively, this recipe will make two individual pies in ramekins with a diameter of about 12 cm/4½ inches.) Pour enough white sauce over to just cover the mixture – you might not need all of it. Give the mixture a gentle toss so the sauce sinks right through to the bottom of the dish.

Gently cover the entire top of the pie with the mashed potato, scraping the mash over the side of the dish as well, so as to seal the top. Scrape a fork over the top of the mash to create a rough texture. Bake for 10–15 minutes, or until the potato topping browns and crisps a little. Serve hot.

SERVES 2

BEER NOTES

La Chouffe is a golden-blonde ale style from the Achouffe Brewery in Belgium, and saison is a French farmhouse-style ale. If you can't find either of these, use a Belgian-style wit beer such as Wicked Elf Witbier, Feral White, Holgate White Ale or Hoegaarden Original White Ale

Indian-style fish curry with Belgian ale

1 teaspoon cumin seeds
1 teaspoon coriander seeds
2 teaspoons black mustard seeds
3 small red chillies, finely chopped
3 garlic cloves, chopped
2.5 cm (1 inch) piece of fresh ginger, chopped

45 ml (1½ fl oz) peanut oil
1 red onion, sliced
1 teaspoon ground turmeric
1 tablespoon curry powder
125 ml (4 fl oz/½ cup) coconut milk
125 ml (4 fl oz/½ cup) coconut cream

250 ml (9 fl oz/1 cup) Belgian-style
   high-alcohol ale
45 ml (1½ fl oz) lemon juice
1 teaspoon grated palm sugar (jaggery)
2 teaspoons fish sauce
10 fresh curry leaves
12 snow peas (mangetout), topped and tailed
12 sugar snap peas, topped and tailed
100 g (3½ oz) baby squid tubes, cut into rings
12 raw prawns (shrimp), peeled and deveined
400 g (14 oz) blue eye cod fillets, cut into
   bite-sized pieces
3 tablespoons chopped fresh coriander (cilantro)

Dry-roast the cumin, coriander and half the mustard seeds in a frying pan over medium heat until fragrant and slightly smoking. Tip into a mortar and grind together to a fine powder using a pestle. Add the chilli, garlic and ginger, along with a pinch of sea salt, then pound until a well-combined paste forms. Set aside.

Heat the oil in a large flameproof casserole dish over medium–high heat. Add the onion and fry, stirring, for 10 minutes or so, until the onion caramelises. Stir in the turmeric, curry powder and remaining mustard seeds and fry for several more minutes until fragrant. Add the spice paste from the mortar and cook over high heat for 10 minutes, stirring to combine all the ingredients and flavours.

Stir in the coconut milk and cream and also the beer. Bring to the boil, then reduce the heat to a simmer. Add the lemon juice, palm sugar, fish sauce and curry leaves. Taste for seasoning, especially the fish sauce, and adjust as needed. Simmer gently for 15 minutes.

Add the snow peas and sugar snap peas and cook for 5 minutes. Gently stir the calamari, prawns and fish through the curry. Poach the seafood for 5–8 minutes, or until just cooked, then stir the chopped coriander through.

Serve over a mixture of cooked jasmine and basmati rice.

SERVES 4

BEER NOTES
Suitable ales
include Leffe Blond,
Red Hill Brewery
Belgian Blonde,
Tuatara Ardennes,
Mad Abbot Dubbel
or Feral Rust

Spanish lentils with chorizo in Belgian ale

a pinch of saffron threads
3 tablespoons olive oil
1 red onion, finely chopped
2 garlic cloves, finely sliced
1 red capsicum (pepper), roughly chopped
300 g (10½ oz) chorizo sausages (the cured variety, rather than fresh), cut in half lengthways, then sliced on the diagonal 1 cm (¼ inch) thick
2 teaspoons smoked paprika
2 dried bay leaves

4 fresh thyme sprigs
2 tomatoes, chopped
two 330 ml (11¼ fl oz) bottles of high-alcohol Belgian ale
500 ml (17 fl oz/2 cups) good-quality chicken stock
2 tablespoons sherry vinegar
375 g (13 oz/2 cups) green lentils
125 g (4½ oz) small button mushrooms, quartered
200 g (7 oz) zucchini (courgettes), finely diced

Steep the saffron threads in 60 ml (2 fl oz/¼ cup) boiling water for 15 minutes.

Meanwhile, heat the olive oil in a saucepan over medium–high heat. When the oil is smoking, add the onion and cook, stirring, for about 5 minutes. Stir in the garlic, capsicum and chorizo and cook for another 5 minutes.

Stir in the paprika, then add the saffron and its soaking liquid and stir it through. Add the bay leaves, thyme, tomato and sea salt to taste. Stir to combine, then cook for several minutes.

Pour in the beer and stock and bring to the boil. Season with freshly ground black pepper, add the sherry vinegar and stir to allow all the flavours to combine. Add the lentils and mix them through while the liquid comes back to the boil. Turn the heat to low, cover with a lid and simmer for 1 hour.

Stir in the mushrooms and zucchini, put the lid back on and simmer for another 45 minutes to 1 hour, or until the lentils are tender but still have a little bite. If you have too much liquid, take the lid off and simmer over a higher heat to reduce it.

Enjoy with a glass of the ale you cooked the lentils with.

SERVES 4

BEER NOTES
Try Westmalle Tripel (9.5%), Hoegaarden Grand Cru (8.5%), Chimay Blue (9%), or Rochefort 8 (9.2%)

Mussels with fennel, leek and dark ale

1 kg (2 lb 4 oz) large mussels – the best mussels
    to buy are locally grown ones; green-lipped
    mussels are gorgeous eating also
25 g (1 oz) unsalted butter
2 tablespoons olive oil

1 leek, mostly white part only, sliced
1 fennel bulb, finely sliced
125 ml (4 fl oz/½ cup) dark ale or lager
440 g (15½ oz) tin chopped tomatoes
2 tablespoons chopped fresh dill

Clean and scrub the mussels, and remove the hairy beards. Set aside.

Heat the butter and olive oil in a large saucepan over medium–low heat. When the butter has melted, add the leek and fennel and gently sweat them for about 5 minutes, or until translucent. Remove from the pan.

Add the beer and then the mussels to the pan, put the lid on and turn the heat to high. Bring to the boil and steam the mussels, shaking the pan once or twice to get the liquid swirling around them. When the mussels have opened (this should take 3–5 minutes), remove the pan from the heat and transfer the mussels to a colander. Discard any mussels that haven't opened.

Strain the cooking liquid over a large bowl to remove any grit and bits of shell, then return the liquid to the pan. Bring to the boil and add the tomatoes, dill and the leek and fennel mixture. Simmer gently for a few minutes to combine the flavours. If the mussels are super fresh they may be full of sea water, which can make this dish quite salty, so make sure you taste the liquid before seasoning with any extra salt. Return the mussels to the pan to warm through.

Serve in big bowls with crusty bread and a spoon to slurp up the fantastic juices.

SERVES 2

BEER NOTES
Try Matilda Bay
Dogbolter Dark
Lager, White Rabbit
Dark Ale, Moo
Brew Dark Ale or
a German dunkel
style ('dunkel' being
German for 'dark')
from brewers such
as Lowenbrau,
Erdinger, Paulaner
or Beck's. Don't
forget to check with
your local micro-
brewery to see if
they are brewing a
dark ale or a dunkel

Ale cassoulet with pork sausage

350 g (12 oz/1¾ cups) dried cannellini beans
80 ml (2½ fl oz/⅓ cup) olive oil
1 onion, chopped
100 g (3½ oz) piece of pancetta, diced
  (if you like a bit of heat, use a chilli pancetta)
3 garlic cloves, chopped
2 carrots, chopped
2 celery stalks, chopped

two 330 ml (11¼ fl oz) bottles of red ale –
  I used Otway Estate Prickly Moses Red Ale,
  or you could use Chimay Red
500 ml (17 fl oz/2 cups) good-quality
  chicken stock
3 fresh rosemary sprigs
4 thick Italian-style pork sausages
2 tablespoons chopped fresh flat-leaf (Italian)
  parsley

Soak the dried beans in a large bowl of cold water overnight. Drain and set aside.

Heat half the olive oil in a large saucepan and add the onion. Cook, stirring, over medium heat until translucent. Add the pancetta and mix through for a few minutes before adding the garlic, carrot and celery. Sweat the vegetables down for about 5 minutes, then add the drained beans and mix through. Pour in equal parts of beer and stock to cover the contents of the pan, then add the rosemary. Simmer, stirring occasionally, for 1½ hours, or until the beans are nearly tender, adding more beer and stock as needed to keep the mixture moist.

Heat the remaining olive oil in a frying pan over medium–high heat. Fry the sausages, browning them on all sides, then remove from the heat. You don't want to cook them, just caramelise the outside.

Add the sausages to the bean mixture, pushing them down into the liquid so they are covered. Simmer the mixture for another 30 minutes, or until the sausages and beans are cooked through. At the end of the cooking time, add sea salt to taste if needed – if you add it earlier the beans will become tough. Mix through some parsley.

Arrange two sausages on each plate and spoon the cassoulet over the top. Garnish with the remaining parsley and serve.

SERVES 2

This is a simple, easy-going risotto that I am sure you will make again and again, so try a different beer each time and see what difference each makes.

Tomato and rocket wheat beer risotto

2 litres (70 fl oz/8 cups) good-quality
    chicken stock
1 tablespoon olive oil
2 tablespoons unsalted butter
1 onion, finely chopped

300 g (10½ oz/1⅓ cups) arborio rice
330 ml (11¼ fl oz) bottle of German wheat beer
1 large handful rocket (arugula)
2 large tomatoes, each cut into eight pieces
25 g (1 oz/¼ cup) finely grated parmesan cheese

Put the stock in a saucepan over high heat and bring to the boil. Turn the heat down to a low simmer.

Heat the olive oil and half the butter in a deep saucepan over medium–low heat. Add the onion and gently sweat until translucent. Add the rice and mix thoroughly, making sure it is well coated with the butter and oil.

Add the beer and stir while the rice absorbs it. Once most of the beer has been absorbed, stir in a ladleful of the simmering stock. When that too has been absorbed, stir in another ladleful of stock and so on for the next 20–30 minutes. If the stock is being absorbed too quickly, turn the heat down; if it's happening too slowly, turn the heat up. Relax, have a beer!

When you have about one ladleful of stock left, or you judge the rice to be close to being done, add the rocket and tomato. (Don't put the rocket and tomato in too early, as you only want to wilt them, not stew them – that way the tomato will hold its shape when served.) Mix them through, then add the last ladleful of stock and stir gently until the rice has absorbed most of the stock and is cooked to your liking. The rice should be al dente: soft on the outside, with a slightly firm bite.

Turn off the heat, add the parmesan and remaining butter and mix through until the ingredients are well combined and the rice has a nice silky texture. Give a grind or two of black pepper and taste for salt. I do this right at the end as the parmesan adds a salty bite to the rice – and if you're using salted butter, that too adds salt. Ladle into bowls and enjoy!

SERVES 4

BEER NOTES
Schofferhofer Hefeweizen, Franziskaner and Erdinger are all imported German wheat beers and very delicious. Aussie versions include Moo Brew Hefeweizen, Redback Original, Bootleg Brewery Sou'West Wheat and Bridge Road Brewers Beechworth Wheat Ale

In the oven

I reckon whoever invented beer must also have invented the oven because they go so well together, especially in the cooler months. But don't be tricked into thinking low and slow means big and stodgy, because it doesn't! It means tender, fragrant and full of flavour, thanks in part to the wonderful addition of all types of beer. It can also mean light and tangy and quite surprising, because cooking with beer often means you need to think outside the square, try something new or put a novel spin on something old. The oven is a great place to do this as baking is a fairly straightforward and safe process when creating one-pot wonders. Just chuck in some meat, vegies, herbs and the appropriate beer, put the lid on, whack it in the oven and leave it for a couple of hours – and hey presto, you have a delicious meal. Just make sure you remember to turn the oven on in the first place!

Beer-braised beef osso bucco

75 g (2½ oz/½ cup) plain (all-purpose) flour
½ teaspoon sea salt
¼ teaspoon freshly ground black pepper
1 teaspoon ground cardamom
4 beef osso bucco pieces
80 ml (2½ fl oz/⅓ cup) olive oil
1 large carrot, diced
3 celery stalks, diced
1 tablespoon capers
2 rosemary sprigs
330 ml (11¼ fl oz) bottle of strong Belgian ale –
    Duvel is one of my all-time favourites and
    is great in this dish

250 ml (9 fl oz/1 cup) good beef or veal stock
2 baby onions, peeled
6 baby potatoes, peeled
400 g (14 oz) jap or kent pumpkin (winter squash),
    skin removed, seeded and cut into
    large cubes
4 Swiss brown mushrooms, quartered
16 green beans, topped and tailed
chopped fresh flat-leaf (Italian) parsley,
    to garnish

Preheat the oven to 170°C (325°F/Gas 3). Put the flour, salt, pepper and cardamom in a clean plastic bag. Add the osso bucco pieces and shake to coat thoroughly.

Heat 3 tablespoons of the olive oil in a flameproof casserole dish over medium–high heat. Brown the osso bucco pieces two at a time and transfer to a plate.

Clean out the casserole dish, as you don't want any burnt-flour character in the finished dish. Heat the remaining olive oil in the dish and fry the carrot and celery for 5 minutes or so. Add the capers and rosemary and cook for 2 minutes. Place the osso bucco pieces on top, then pour in the beer and stock. Bring to the boil, cover with a lid and place in the oven. Bake for 1 hour.

Add the onions, potatoes, pumpkin and mushrooms and stir them in so they are submerged in the cooking liquid. Put the lid back on and bake for a further 45 minutes to 1 hour – the longer and slower the better. When the meat is very tender, add the beans and cook for 8–10 minutes.

Transfer the osso bucco and vegetables from the pan to a large bowl and keep warm. Put the dish back on the stovetop over high heat and reduce the liquid to a nice sauce consistency. Season to taste with sea salt and freshly ground black pepper.

Divide the vegetables among serving plates. Place the osso bucco on top of the vegetables, then generously drizzle the sauce over the meat and around the plate. Garnish with the parsley and serve.

SERVES 2–4

Dark ale-braised oxtail and rabbit pappardelle

150 g (5½ oz/1 cup) plain (all-purpose) flour
1 kg (2 lb 4 oz) oxtail pieces
1 rabbit, cut into 6 pieces (I use farmed rabbit as
　　this is what most butchers and delis sell;
　　it is also easier to cook than wild rabbit)
45 g (1½ oz) unsalted butter
3 tablespoons olive oil
2 carrots, finely diced
2 celery stalks, finely diced
100 g (3½ oz) pancetta, cut into 5 mm x 1 cm
　　(¼ x ½ inch) strips
10 French shallots, peeled and quartered

6 garlic cloves, roughly chopped
60 g (2¼ oz/¼ cup) chopped tomatoes,
　　fresh or tinned
3 dried bay leaves
½ tablespoon chopped fresh thyme
½ tablespoon chopped fresh marjoram
1 cinnamon stick
500 ml (17 fl oz/2 cups) White Rabbit Dark Ale
350 ml (12 fl oz) good beef stock
400 g (14 oz) pappardelle pasta
235 g (8½ oz/1½ cups) fresh or frozen peas
finely chopped fresh flat-leaf parsley, to garnish

Preheat the oven to 170°C (325°F/Gas 3).

Put the flour in a clean plastic bag and season well with sea salt and freshly ground black pepper. Shake to combine. Put the oxtail and rabbit pieces in the bag and give it a really good shake to coat the meat well.

Heat the butter and olive oil in a flameproof casserole dish over high heat. Add the oxtail and rabbit pieces and brown them on all sides. Remove the meat from the dish and set aside.

Turn the heat down to medium. Add the carrot and celery and cook, stirring, for several minutes. Now add the pancetta, shallots and garlic and cook, stirring often, for about 8 minutes. Stir in the tomatoes, bay leaves, thyme, marjoram and cinnamon stick and cook for 5 minutes.

Place the oxtail and rabbit in the dish on top of the other ingredients and pour in the beer and stock. Bring to the boil, then remove from the heat.

Take a sheet of baking paper and cut out a piece that will fit snugly on top of the braise to cover it completely. Butter one side of the baking paper (or spray it with olive oil spray), then place that side down on top of the braise, gently pressing it to give a good seal. Put a lid on the dish and place in the oven. After the first hour turn the meat, cover with the baking paper again and bake for a further 1½–2 hours. You will know the meat is done because the oxtail will be falling off the bone; the rabbit won't, but you should be able to pull it apart with a fork.

Remove the meat from the dish and place it in a bowl to catch any juices while waiting for it to cool down. When the meat is cool enough to handle, pull all the meat off the bones and shred it. At this point you can also discard some of the oxtail fat if you don't want to eat it. Put the meat back in the bowl with the juices.

Bring a large saucepan of salted water to the boil, then add the pasta.

Meanwhile, put the dish with the braising vegies over medium–high heat and bring to a simmer. Remove the cinnamon stick, add the peas and simmer until the liquid has reduced to the consistency of a pasta sauce. If for any reason the mixture has come out of the oven too dry, add a little beef stock to bring it up to the right consistency – bear in mind that you'll be adding the shredded meat, which will thicken the sauce a little more. Taste for salt and freshly ground black pepper and adjust if needed. Add the shredded meat and keep it on a low heat while the pasta cooks.

When the pasta is al dente, use tongs to transfer it straight into the braise – any water clinging to the pasta will help to moisten the sauce a little. Give it all a really good toss to coat the pasta. Divide among six bowls, garnish with parsley and serve.

SERVES 6

BEER NOTES

White Rabbit Dark Ale is a unique Australian beer as it is made using an open fermentation process, which very few breweries around the world still practise. This gives the beer a lovely yeast profile that works very well with the rabbit, as does the roasted dark malt character in this ale. If you can't get White Rabbit, use another dark ale such as Coopers Dark Ale, 3 Ravens Dark, Red Hill Brewery Scotch Ale or Tooheys Old, or drop by your local micro-brewery and see if they can give you some of their dark ale off the tap

Lamb and beer curry

2 tablespoons peanut oil
1 red onion, sliced
2.5 cm (1 inch) piece of fresh ginger, chopped
3 garlic cloves, finely chopped
1 teaspoon chopped fresh turmeric
1 red chilli, finely sliced
1 teaspoon cardamom seeds
1 teaspoon lemongrass powder
2 tablespoons red curry paste

700 g (1 lb 9 oz) lamb leg, no bone, cut into 4 cm
   (1½ inch) chunks
125 g (4½ oz/½ cup) plain yoghurt
330 ml (11¼ fl oz) bottle of Moonshine Ale (8%)
   from Grand Ridge Brewery
3 potatoes, peeled and each cut into six pieces
1 large handful fresh coriander (cilantro), chopped
16 sugar snap peas, topped and tailed
16 green beans, topped and tailed

Preheat the oven to 170°C (325°F/Gas 3).

Heat the oil in a flameproof casserole dish over medium heat. Add the onion and cook, stirring often, until lightly caramelised. Add the ginger, garlic, turmeric and chilli and cook, stirring, for 5 minutes.

Stir in the cardamom seeds and lemongrass powder and cook for a few minutes more. Stir in the curry paste and cook until fragrant, then add the lamb pieces and stir well to thoroughly coat all the lamb with the paste. Stir in the yoghurt, bring to a simmer, then add the beer, stirring well to combine. Bring back to a simmer.

Put the lid on the dish, place in the oven and bake for 45 minutes. Stir in the potato and 2 tablespoons of the coriander, then replace the lid and bake for another 30–40 minutes – the meat should be quite tender by now.

Add the sugar snap peas and beans and bake, still covered, for a final 5 minutes. Stir the remaining coriander through just before serving.

SERVES 4

BEER NOTES

You could also try a high-alcohol Belgian-style ale from your local micro-brewery, such as Feral Rust, the Mad Abbot range from The Little Brewing Company, or Red Hill Brewery Temptation or Belgian Blonde

Saison is one of my favourite styles of beer. Light, sweet, spicy and effervescent, it is a great beer, not only to drink but to cook with, too. And two of my favourite Australian saisons are Temple Saison and Bridge Road Brewers Chevalier Saison. The world-renowned Saison Dupont is also a fabulous beer and well worth finding. Another beer that technically isn't a saison but has many similarities is La Chouffe – it, too, is one of my favourites to drink and to cook with.

Coconut and ale-braised pickled pork

200 ml (7 fl oz) coconut cream
200 ml (7 fl oz) coconut milk
250 ml (9 fl oz/1 cup) saison ale
1 lemongrass stem, white part only
3 cm (1¼ inch) piece of fresh ginger, peeled
4 makrut (kaffir lime) leaves
1 long red chilli, finely sliced into rounds

2 teaspoons fish sauce
1 tablespoon grated palm sugar (jaggery)
600 g (1 lb 5 oz) pickled pork, cut into large chunks
10 snow peas (mangetout), topped and tailed
10 sugar snap peas, topped and tailed

Preheat the oven to 160°C (315°F/Gas 2–3).

Heat the coconut cream, coconut milk and beer in a flameproof casserole dish over medium heat. Give the lemongrass a bash with a rolling pin or the flat side of a knife blade to break it open, then add to the dish. Bash the ginger as well and add it to the dish. Throw in the lime leaves, chilli, fish sauce and palm sugar and slowly bring the sauce to a simmer. Taste for seasoning and a balance between the ginger, fish sauce, chilli and palm sugar.

Add the pork and bring back to a gentle simmer. Put the lid on, transfer to the oven and bake for about 2 hours. The meat should be very fragrant, slightly salty and very tender. The saltiness of pickled pork will vary between butchers, as some are more heavy-handed with the salt than others. When you find a butcher that salts their pork to your liking, stick with them!

Add the snow peas and sugar snap peas and cook until they are tender, about 3 minutes. Ladle the stew and lots of the broth over bowls of rice and serve with a nice glass of saison.

SERVES 3–4

Shoulder of baby goat braised in milk, saison and Mexican chillies

plain (all-purpose) flour, for dredging
1 shoulder of baby goat, weighing 1.2–1.5 kg
    (2 lb 10 oz–3 lb 5 oz), cut in two at the
    middle joint
1 tablespoon olive oil
250 ml (9 fl oz/1 cup) milk
250 ml (9 fl oz/1 cup) saison ale
1½ tablespoons honey

CHILLI PASTE
1 head of garlic
1–2 teaspoons olive oil
3 chipotle (dried smoked jalapeño) chillies
4 pasilla chillies
4 guajillo chillies

250 ml (9 fl oz/1 cup) boiling water
1 teaspoon finely chopped fresh thyme
1 teaspoon finely chopped fresh marjoram
½ teaspoon ground cumin
¼ teaspoon ground white pepper
½ teaspoon sea salt

SALSA
1 red onion, finely diced
2 tomatoes, skin and seeds removed, flesh diced
1 avocado, diced
1–2 tablespoons finely chopped fresh coriander
    (cilantro)
juice of ½ lime

Preheat the oven to 200°C (400°F/Gas 6). To make the chilli paste, place the whole head of garlic on a sheet of foil that has been folded in half. Drizzle with the olive oil, sprinkle with sea salt and wrap the garlic up. Bake for 20–30 minutes, until the garlic is nice and soft. Remove from the oven and leave to cool.

Cut the top part of the chillies off, removing the stems. Shake out all the seeds, then cut each chilli into three or four pieces, depending on their size – the chipotles you can just cut in half.

Put a frying pan over medium–high heat and place half the chilli pieces in the pan – don't overlap them as you want to toast the skins. Cover them with another frying pan or a heavy stewing pot to press the chillies down so the skins are in contact with the hot surface. Toast for a couple of minutes, until the chillies smell fragrant and begin to smoke a little – be careful not to burn them! Remove the top pan or pot, turn the chillies over and toast the other side, again weighing them down. Transfer to a large bowl and repeat the toasting process with the remaining chillies, adding them to the bowl. Pour the boiling water over the chillies, so that they're all covered, then place a bowl on top of them to push them under the water. Soak for 30 minutes.

Drain the chillies, reserving the soaking liquid. Put the chillies in a food processor, along with about 125 ml (4 fl oz/½ cup) of the soaking liquid. Squeeze out the garlic flesh from each roasted clove and add to the processor with the thyme, marjoram, cumin, white pepper and salt. Process to form a rough sauce, stopping once or twice to scrape down the sides of the bowl. If the sauce is too thick, add a little more of the soaking liquid – it should be a bit like a runny porridge. Once it is well blended, pour the sauce into a sieve that is resting over a bowl. Then, using a soft spatula, push the sauce through the sieve, discarding all the solids left behind.

Heat the oven to 160°C (315°F/Gas 2–3). Put the flour in a clean plastic bag and season with sea salt and freshly ground black pepper. Add the goat and shake the bag, then shake off the excess.

Heat the olive oil in a large flameproof casserole dish or baking dish over medium–high heat and brown the goat all over. Turn the heat down to medium and stir in the chilli paste. Cook for several minutes, turning the goat so that it is well covered by the paste. (At this point you could, if you like, marinate the goat overnight.) Add the milk and beer. Stir to combine, bring back to a gentle boil, then add the honey and stir again for a minute or two.

Cover the casserole dish with a tight-fitting lid, transfer to the oven and bake for 2–2½ hours, turning the goat over after the first hour, and taking the lid off for the last 20 minutes. The goat will be falling-off-the-bone tender and moist.

Just before serving, mix the salsa ingredients in a bowl with a pinch of sea salt.

To serve the goat Mexican style, pull the meat off the bone, shred it with two forks and put it on a plate. Serve it up with the salsa, some roasted corn cut off the cob, a bowl of the sauce from the casserole dish and some fresh steamed tortillas. Tear off some of the tortilla, wrap it around some meat, salsa, corn and sauce, then eat it! If you haven't already, drink the rest of the beer you used in the cooking – and if you already have, then open another one.

SERVES 4

BEER NOTES

Saison ale is also known as 'seasonal' ale; Aussie versions include Temple Saison, Otway Estate Prickly Moses Saison and Bridge Road Brewers Chevalier Saison. Also try the Belgian-made Saison Dupont, voted the world's best beer in 2005

Veal gueuze casserole

25 g (1 oz) unsalted butter

2 tablespoons olive oil, plus extra for pan-frying,
    if needed

1 large leek, white part only, sliced

2 garlic cloves, chopped

35 g (1¼ oz/¼ cup) plain (all-purpose) flour

700 g (1 lb 9 oz) boned veal, cut into 4 cm
    (1½ inch) chunks

70 g (2½ oz) good fatty speck, finely sliced

1 teaspoon ground cumin

1 teaspoon ground coriander

½ teaspoon ground cardamom

two 330 ml (11¼ fl oz) bottles of gueuze ale

250 ml (9 fl oz/1 cup) good chicken stock

110 g (3¾ oz/½ cup) pearl barley

2 carrots, roughly chopped

zest of 1 lemon

3 tablespoons fresh flat-leaf (Italian) parsley

PAN-FRIED HERBS

25 g (1 oz) unsalted butter

3 tablespoons chopped fresh mint

3 tablespoons chopped fresh flat-leaf (Italian)
    parsley

BEER NOTES

Gueuze (which is pronounced *gooz-eh*) – is a Belgian specialty from the early 1500s. It is made in the lambic style and is a blend of one-year-old and three-year-old lambic. It is sweet, sour, quite tart and effervescent – a 'champagne' type of beer. Brands we can buy in Australia include Timmermans, Lindeman's, Mort Subite, Cantillon and Belle-Vue

Preheat the oven to 170°C (325°F/Gas 3).

Heat the butter and olive oil in a large flameproof casserole dish over medium heat. When the butter foams, add the leek and sweat it for 5 minutes. Add the garlic and cook for another 3 minutes. Remove the mixture from the pan and keep warm.

Season the flour well with plenty of sea salt and freshly ground black pepper. Use it to coat the veal, shaking off any excess. Add a little more olive oil to the pan if needed, increase the heat to high and brown the veal – you may need to do this in two batches. Add the speck and fry with the veal for 4–5 minutes, then return the leek and garlic to the pan. Add the cumin, coriander and cardamom and mix through well; cook for several minutes.

Add half the gueuze and deglaze the dish, using a wooden spoon to scrape all the yummy bits off the bottom. Add the remaining gueuze and the stock and bring to the boil, stirring all the time. Turn the heat down to a simmer. Add the barley, stirring it through while bringing the liquid back to a simmer. Place a lid on the casserole and put it in the oven. Bake for 1 hour.

When the veal has been in the oven for nearly an hour, pan-fry the herbs. Melt the butter in a small frying pan and when hot, add the mint and parsley. Fry over medium heat for about 7 minutes, stirring often.

Stir the fried herbs through the veal, then add the carrot. Taste for seasoning and add sea salt and freshly ground black pepper if needed. Put the lid back on and return to the oven for 30–40 minutes more, or until the veal is very tender.

Very finely chop together the lemon zest and remaining parsley. Serve the veal garnished with the lemon zest mixture.

SERVES 4

Okay, this is a very simple dish, and like all simple dishes it relies on really good produce. Here it is all about the sausages, so please buy some very good gourmet-type snags. I love pork and fennel sausages and also love hot Italian sausages (salsicce). Actually, I love any good sausage! Boerewors, the South African sausage you see in butcher shops packaged up in a coil, would also be great in this dish. The spicy flavours from the sausages, the sweetness from the onions and the lovely malty character of the beer all mix together beautifully. Add the sweetness from the peas and the carrot and their slightly crunchy texture and it all adds up to make this a surprisingly good dish!

Surprisingly good beer-braised sausages and peas

3 tablespoons olive oil
2 pork and fennel sausages
2 hot Italian sausages (or mild, if you don't like
   that chilli bite)

3 onions, sliced
three 330 ml (11¼ fl oz) bottles of pilsner
235 g (8½ oz/1½ cups) frozen peas
1 large carrot, diced

Preheat the oven to 160°C (315°F/Gas 2–3).

Heat most of the olive oil in a large flameproof casserole dish over medium–high heat. Add the sausages and brown on all sides. Remove from the dish and set aside.

Heat the rest of the olive oil in the dish. Add the onion and cook, stirring, for a couple of minutes, then turn the heat down and cook gently for about 10 minutes, until the onion is caramelised.

Return the sausages to the dish, then pour in enough beer to cover the sausages – if you don't use all of it I suggest you drink what is left over! Put a lid on the dish and place it in the oven. Bake for 2 hours.

Just before serving, cook the peas and carrots together, either in the microwave, in some simmering salted water, or by steaming them – don't overcook as you want a little bit of crunch from them. Drain and divide evenly between two plates.

Place one of each sausage on top of the peas and carrots, then spoon the beer broth and onion over. Eat!

You could also serve a lovely creamy potato mash with this if you wanted.

SERVES 2

BEER NOTES
I used Blue Tongue Traditional Pilsner. You could also use Red Angus Pilsener, Cricketers Arms Lager or of course Peroni Nastro Azzurro. You could also try using a Mountain Goat Steam Ale

When you buy octopus from your fishmonger, it will usually have been tumbled to tenderise it, and the skin will have been removed, so all you need to do is give it a wash to clean out any sand lurking in the sucker pads. Octopus differs from red meat in that it doesn't require long cooking to become tender. You can tell when it is cooked in the same way you check whether your boiled potatoes are cooked – insert a knife tip into the thickest part, and if it meets no resistance it is done.

Slow-braised octopus

½ fennel bulb, sliced
½ red onion, sliced
1 chorizo sausage, sliced
1 large octopus leg, about 350 g (12 oz)
3 tablespoons olive oil
500 ml (17 fl oz/2 cups) dark German wheat
    beer (dunkel), such as Weihenstephaner
    Dunkel, Erdinger Dunkel or Franziskaner

3 long, fresh rosemary sprigs
8 cherry tomatoes
chopped fresh flat-leaf (Italian) parsley, to garnish

Place the fennel, onion and chorizo in a baking dish. Put the octopus leg on top, drizzle with the olive oil, then pour in the beer. Season with plenty of freshly ground black pepper and add the rosemary. Do not salt the octopus as it will be salty anyway, and added salt may toughen it during cooking. Mix with your hands so that everything gets nicely combined and well coated. Using a sharp knife, make a small cross in the bottom of each cherry tomato and scatter them around the dish. Cover the dish and marinate for a couple of hours, or overnight.

Preheat the oven to 170°C (325°F/Gas 3). Remove the dish from the fridge and allow it to come to room temperature. Cover the dish tightly with foil, then prick the foil once to allow steam to escape. Bake until the octopus is fork-tender – this should take about 45 minutes, or up to 1 hour at the most.

Cut thin slices from the octopus leg and arrange on a plate. Dress with the fennel, onion, chorizo and tomatoes from the dish and spoon some of the cooking juices over. Garnish with the parsley and serve.

SERVES 2

I have made this dish a lot as it is one of my favourites, and I've used quite a few different beers along the way – both ales and lagers. I have to say, though, that I think the Belgian ale known as Duvel is the best beer for this dish. Rumour has it that it takes ninety days to make this beer: compare that to your mass-made Aussie pilsner, which takes about seven days, and you just know it has to be great! Its high alcohol content works well with the sweetness of the pork, its malty character marries well with the heat from the red curry paste, and the hop character cuts the coconut cream, so the whole dish is fresh, fragrant, clean and delicious.

Pork and pumpkin red curry

3 tablespoons peanut oil

1 red onion, halved and sliced

½ red capsicum (pepper), cut into thin strips

3 tablespoons Thai red curry paste

700 g (1 lb 9 oz) pork neck, cut into 4–5 cm (1½–2 inch) cubes (I like my curry meat to be in big chunks)

1 tablespoon tamarind pulp, soaked in 60 ml (2 fl oz/¼ cup) boiling water

270 ml (9½ fl oz) coconut cream

330 ml (11¼ fl oz) bottle of Duvel – a spectacular Belgian ale that is fruity, clean and unique

4 makrut (kaffir lime) leaves

500 g (1 lb 2 oz) pumpkin (winter squash), peeled and cut into 3 cm (1 inch) chunks

3 potatoes, peeled and cut into 8 pieces each

8 baby (pattypan) squash, cut in half

2 zucchini (courgettes), cut into rounds

1 handful fresh coriander (cilantro), chopped

sliced red chilli, to serve (optional)

Preheat the oven to 180°C (350°F/Gas 4).

Heat the oil in a large flameproof casserole dish over medium–high heat. Sweat the onion and capsicum until just starting to colour. Stir in the curry paste and cook for several minutes, until fragrant and well combined.

Add the pork and mix well to coat with the sauce, then cook over high heat for a few minutes, stirring all the time. Stir in the strained tamarind liquor, then add the coconut cream and beer, giving it all a good stir to combine. Bring up to a boil before adding the lime leaves, pumpkin and potato. Stir all the vegetables through and again let the mixture come up to a boil. Turn off the heat, put a lid on the dish and transfer it to the oven. Bake for 1½ hours, giving the stew a stir once or twice.

Add the squash and zucchini and bake for a further 45 minutes, depending on how you like your vegies done. During cooking the pumpkin will break down completely, mixing with all the cooking juices to make a rich pumpkin sauce!

Stir some of the coriander through. Serve the curry in big bowls on a bed of rice, garnished with the remaining coriander, and chilli slices if desired.

SERVES 4

Rabbit and stout casserole

25 g (1 oz) unsalted butter
2 tablespoons olive oil
1 leek, white part only, thickly sliced
3 carrots, thickly sliced
1 farmed rabbit, cut into six pieces
2 tablespoons plain (all-purpose) flour
250 ml (9 fl oz/1 cup) Coopers Best Extra Stout
3 dried bay leaves
5 fresh sage leaves

1 tablespoon chopped fresh rosemary
225 g (8 oz/1 cup) pitted prunes

GARLIC MASH
3 potatoes, peeled and chopped
2–3 garlic cloves, crushed
50 g (1¾ oz) unsalted butter
a splash or two of milk

BEER NOTES

I love Coopers Best Extra Stout with this dish. Its deep, roasted-malt character works well with the rabbit and the high bitterness is tempered by the sweetness of the prunes. Other stouts will work fine, such as Red Hill Brewery Imperial Stout or Moo Brew Imperial Stout, but do yourself a favour and try it with the Coopers first

Preheat the oven to 180°C (350°F/Gas 4).

Heat the butter and olive oil in a flameproof casserole dish over medium–high heat. When the butter is foaming, add the leek and carrot. Sweat for 5 minutes, or until the leek is translucent, then remove from the dish and set aside.

Season the rabbit pieces with a little sea salt and freshly ground black pepper and brown them in the dish, adding a little more oil if needed. Once the rabbit is browned all over, remove from the dish and keep warm.

Add the flour to the dish and cook for 2 minutes, stirring and scraping vigorously. Add 170 ml (5½ fl oz/⅔ cup) water and continue to stir and scrape vigorously until the sauce thickens. Stir in the beer and bay leaves and bring to the boil. Return the rabbit to the dish, add the sage and rosemary, then the leek and carrot mixture, giving them a bit of a stir. Cover the dish and bake for 40 minutes.

Stir the prunes through and bake, still covered, for a further 40 minutes, or until the rabbit is very tender. Be careful not to overcook the rabbit or it will become dry.

When the rabbit is nearly done, make the garlic mash. Cook the potatoes in a saucepan of salted boiling water until tender, then drain and return to the pan. Place the garlic in a heatproof bowl with the butter. Heat in a microwave until the butter has melted, then add to the potato with a little milk. Mash over low heat until creamy and smooth, then season with sea salt and freshly ground black pepper.

Serve the casserole with the garlic mash, steamed snake (yard-long) beans and a large glass of Coopers stout.

SERVES 4

Boston-style beer-baked beans

125 g (4½ oz) dried pinto beans
125 g (4½ oz) dried red kidney beans
125 g (4½ oz) dried great northern beans
3 tablespoons olive oil
1 onion, chopped
2 garlic cloves, finely sliced
a pinch of ground cloves
2 teaspoons mustard powder
2 teaspoons smoked paprika

¼ teaspoon chilli flakes
95 g (3¼ oz/½ cup) brown sugar
440 g (15½ oz) tin chopped tomatoes
1 teaspoon worcestershire sauce
3 tablespoons maple syrup
250 ml (9 fl oz/1 cup) Leffe Radieuse
400 g (14 oz) piece of bacon, cut into four equal
    slices about 1.5 cm (⅝ inch) thick

Put the dried beans in a large bowl and cover with plenty of cold water. Leave overnight and drain just before you need to use them.

Preheat the oven to 160ºC (315ºF/Gas 2–3).

Heat the olive oil in a flameproof casserole dish over medium–high heat. Add the onion and fry, stirring, for about 5 minutes, or until translucent. Add the garlic and stir for several minutes. Now add the cloves, mustard powder, paprika and chilli flakes, stirring to combine well. Stir in the sugar, tomatoes, worcestershire sauce, maple syrup, beer and 250 ml (9 fl oz/1 cup) water. Bring to the boil, add the bacon and drained beans and mix well.

Cut a piece of baking paper to fit snugly on top of the stew. Place the paper directly on top of the stew, then put the lid on. Transfer to the oven and bake for 3 hours, or until the beans are tender. Halfway through cooking, check the liquid: if it has been fully absorbed, add equal amounts of water and beer so that the beans do not become too dry. Check again in 45–60 minutes.

Check for seasoning and add some sea salt and freshly ground black pepper as necessary. To serve, spoon a ladleful of beans onto a plate, sit a piece of bacon on top, then spoon a little more of the bean mixture over the bacon.

SERVES 4

BEER NOTES
Leffe Radieuse is a delicious Belgian Abbey beer with a high alcohol content and a red colour. It marries well with the bacon flavour and maple syrup sweetness

You cannot write a beer cookbook without doing a slow-cooked lamb and Guinness dish – so here is mine!

Lamb shanks in Guinness

75 g (2½ oz/½ cup) plain (all-purpose) flour
½ teaspoon sea salt
½ teaspoon freshly ground black pepper
½ teaspoon ground cardamom
½ teaspoon ground cumin
1 teaspoon cayenne pepper
2 good, meaty lamb shanks
3 tablespoons olive oil
8 French shallots, peeled
1 large carrot, cut on the diagonal into 1 cm
   (½ inch) slices

4 garlic cloves
2 fresh lemon thyme sprigs
2 dried bay leaves
12 kalamata olives
1 tomato, peeled and chopped
1 lemon peel strip, white pith removed
375 ml (13 fl oz/1½ cups) Guinness or other stout
250 ml (9 fl oz/1 cup) good beef stock
3 kipfler (fingerling) potatoes, cut into 2 cm
   (¾ inch) slices
24 green beans, topped and tailed

Preheat the oven to 180°C (350°F/Gas 4).

Put the flour, salt, black pepper, cardamom, cumin and cayenne pepper in a clean plastic bag and give it a good toss to combine. Add the shanks, twist the top around to seal, then give the bag another good shake to coat the shanks well. Remove the shanks from the bag, gently hit them together to knock off the excess flour, then set aside.

Heat the olive oil in a flameproof casserole dish over high heat. Add the shanks and brown on all sides. Add the shallots, carrot and garlic and cook for several minutes to colour them. Add the lemon thyme, bay leaves, olives, tomato and lemon peel. Stir to combine, then cook for about 5 minutes.

Stir in the stout and stock and bring to the boil. Put a lid on the dish, transfer to the oven and bake for 1 hour. Turn the shanks over and add the potatoes, then bake, covered, for another 1 hour.

Remove the lid, add the beans and cook for 5 minutes, or until the beans are cooked to your liking. The sauce should by now have reduced to a nice consistency, but if it hasn't, transfer the shanks and vegetables to a large bowl and leave them in the turned-off oven to keep warm. Place the dish over medium–high heat and reduce the sauce to the desired consistency, then return the shanks and vegetables to the dish and mix well so they are all coated with the sauce.

SERVES 2

BEER NOTES
Other stouts you could use here include Mountain Goat Surefoot Stout, Nail Brewing Company Nail Stout, Coopers Best Extra Stout or Moo Brew Imperial Stout – there are lots of good stouts being made out there!

Fragrant Hoegaarden fish parcels

1 tablespoon unsalted butter, softened

1 handful baby spinach leaves

3 French shallots, peeled and finely sliced

1 lemongrass stem, white part only, halved lengthways and smashed into pieces with the back of a knife blade

4 lemon slices

2 blue eye cod fillets, 180–225 g (6–8 oz) each, without skin

½ carrot, finely julienned

¼ red capsicum (pepper), finely julienned

8 green beans, topped and tailed, then halved lengthways

4 cherry tomatoes, quartered

2 tablespoons chopped fresh coriander (cilantro)

12 fresh basil leaves

olive oil, for drizzling

330 ml (11¼ fl oz) bottle of Belgian wit ale

BEER NOTES

I use the Belgian wit ('white ale') in this dish because it is brewed with coriander (cilantro) and orange peel, which works well here; it is also a wheat beer, which adds a softness to the sauce that is created during baking. Hoegaarden Witbier is the grand champion of this style and is perfect for this dish. Australian versions include Feral White, Holgate White Ale, 3 Ravens White Witbier and Bright Brewery Razor Witbier

Preheat the oven to 190°C (375°F/Gas 5).

Take two sheets of foil about 40 cm (16 inches) long and lay them shiny side down on the work surface next to each other. Tear off two more sheets and place these on top of the first ones, again shiny side down. These will become your parcels, and obviously you are making two – one for you and one for your sweetheart.

Using your fingers, smear the butter over the middle section of each of the foil sheets, making it longer than it is wide and roughly duplicating the size of the fish fillets. Now layer the rest of the ingredients over the butter, dividing them equally between the two parcels. The order is: spinach, shallot, lemongrass, lemon slices, fish, carrot, capsicum, beans, tomato, coriander, basil, a sprinkle of sea salt and freshly ground black pepper, a drizzle of olive oil, and finally about 2–3 tablespoons of the beer over each stack.

Now make the foil parcels by taking the two long sides and bringing them up and over the fish so they meet, then folding them over each other several times to seal all the way along. Then fold over the two shorter ends to seal, folding and wrapping them over until they are snug against the ingredients inside. The parcels should be of a similar shape to the fish and tightly sealed.

Place the parcels on a baking tray and bake for about 20 minutes. Check the fish after 15 minutes by carefully unwrapping a middle section of the parcel and poking the fish with a fork – if it flakes easily, it is done. Obviously the cooking time will depend on the thickness of the fillets, so be careful not to overcook the fish or it will become tough.

Serve each parcel on a plate, allowing the diner to open the parcel and eat directly out of it to enjoy the aromas, the fish and vegetables – and of course the broth!

SERVES 2

Meatloaf

7 long bacon slices
300 g (10½ oz) minced (ground) beef
300 g (10½ oz) minced (ground) veal
200 g (7 oz) minced (ground) pork
1 onion, finely diced
3 garlic cloves, finely crushed
2 free-range eggs
75 g (2½ oz/¾ cup) rolled (porridge) oats
2 tablespoons tomato sauce (ketchup)
1 tablespoon worcestershire sauce
1 teaspoon Tabasco sauce (optional)

1 carrot, grated
3 celery stalks, grated
125 ml (4 fl oz/½ cup) porter, such as James
    Squire Porter, Tuatara Porter, Lord Nelson Old
    Admiral or a locally made micro-brewed porter
½ teaspoon ground cumin
1 teaspoon smoked paprika
1 teaspoon ground fennel
1 teaspoon sea salt
½ teaspoon freshly ground black pepper
½ teaspoon dried mixed herbs

Preheat the oven to 180°C (350°F/Gas 4).

Lightly oil a loaf (bar) tin measuring 21 cm (8¼ inches) long, 11 cm (4¼ inches) wide and 7 cm (3 inches) deep, or do what I do and use a traditional bread baking tin. Line the tin with the bacon slices. Start from one end of the tin and lay the rashers crossways, touching, so that their ends hang over the sides of the tin. Push them together so there are no spaces in between. Use the last two slices to line each end of the tin, leaving a long tail for folding back down the loaf's length.

Combine the remaining ingredients in a large bowl, mixing them thoroughly. Take a teaspoon of the mixture and fry it in a small non-stick frying pan in a tiny amount of olive oil. This is your tester, so when it's cooked, taste it for seasoning and adjust the meatloaf mixture to your liking if necessary. Fill the tin with the mixture, patting it down firmly. Fold the bacon slices over the filling in the same order as you laid them down, ending with the two slices running end to end. Tuck the ends down between the meatloaf and the tin – you will now have a very neatly wrapped package in a bread tin!

Bake for 1 hour, draining off any excess juice every 20 minutes or so. Remove from the oven and carefully turn the meatloaf out onto a baking tray. Turn the oven up to 200°C (400°F/Gas 6) and put the loaf back in for 20 minutes to brown the bacon. If you have a meat thermometer, stick it into the meatloaf in the mid-section. The meatloaf is cooked when the temperature reads 80°C (175°F).

Cut the meatloaf into thick slices and serve two per person. Serve with mashed potatoes, steamed brussels sprouts and some of my hot and spicy barbecue sauce (see page 149). It is also great cold the next day for lunch!

SERVES 6–8

From the grill

There really is nothing like cooking over hot coals or gas-driven flames, is there? I don't know what it is that draws you to stand silently next to the barbecue, mesmerised by the flames as they reach out and gently caress your perfectly seasoned steak. I love the symphony of sounds that rise from the grill as your sausages pop, your chicken sizzles and your corn on the cob explodes – intermittently accompanied by the glorious sound of the top being prised from the bottle of your favourite brew, of course! I love cooking on the barbecue at night as the glow from the flames acts like a beacon for people to gather around in silence, needing nothing more than the sight, the sounds and the smells coming from the barbecue. It truly is a diverse way of cooking – if it has a lid it doubles as an oven, without a lid it's a stovetop, and all the while it imparts that wonderful smoky flavour to your food, not to mention the lovely caramelised chargrilled crust that only a flame or hot coals can give.

I have a traditional paella pan that fits snugly on my Weber kettle barbecue. When I make my paella I drop pieces of hickory wood onto the hot coals, which creates lots of smoke, then I close the lid and let the smoke sink into the rice as it bubbles away – magnificent! If you can, cook this paella over a fire as the results are well worth the effort. In fact the paella pan was designed to encourage the smoke to come up the sides of the pan and into the dish itself.

Pilsner paella with quail, chorizo and seafood

3 tablespoons olive oil

1 tablespoon smoked paprika

3 garlic cloves, finely chopped

3 quails, boned and quartered – or use 6 boneless chicken thighs

2 chorizo sausages, sliced 5 mm (¼ inch) thick on the diagonal

8 chipolata pork sausages

1 red capsicum (pepper), finely sliced

1 small red chilli, finely sliced (or as much or as little as you want)

440 g (15½ oz/2 cups) short-grain rice, such as arborio or calasparra

440 g (15½ oz) tin chopped tomatoes

a pinch of saffron threads, soaked in a little warm water

330 ml (11¼ fl oz) bottle of pilsner

1.25 litres (44 fl oz/5 cups) chicken stock

250 g (9 oz) scallops (roe on or off, as you prefer)

10 raw prawns (shrimp)

10 mussels

155 g (5½ oz/1 cup) frozen peas

150 g (5½ oz) green beans, topped and tailed, then cut into thirds

Preheat the barbecue to high. Place your paella pan over the coals or flames and in it heat most of the olive oil. Add the paprika and half the garlic, and when the garlic starts to sizzle add the quail, chorizo and chipolatas. Stir so they are well coated with the oil and the paprika, and fry until just nicely coloured. Remove all the meat from the pan and keep warm.

Add the rest of the oil to the pan, then add the remaining garlic, the capsicum and chilli and cook until the capsicum has softened. Stir in the rice, ensuring it is well coated with the oil. Add the tomatoes and mix well, allowing the rice to absorb the liquid from the tomatoes, then add the saffron and its soaking water, then the beer. Stir to combine the flavours and to help the rice soak up the beer.

When all the beer has been absorbed and the rice has become dry, 4–6 minutes, stir in a cup of stock. Traditionally you are not supposed to stir a paella, just add all the stock and let it cook away, but I tend to do my paella a little more like a risotto – add some stock, give it a stir and let the rice soak it up, then add another ladle, give it a stir, and so on. Just like cooking any rice dish, you don't want it to cook too quickly or too slowly, so keep an eye on it. When you have used about three-quarters of your stock, add the scallops, prawns, mussels, peas and beans, then another ladle of stock. Give the rice a stir and let it absorb the liquid. Check for seasoning.

Push the warm quail, chorizo and sausages into the rice. Add the last of the stock, then cover and cook for about 8 minutes – with no more stirring – until the rice is the texture and consistency you like (not too dry, nor too moist). At this stage a golden caramelised crust called a socarrat will form on the bottom of the pan – in Spain this is considered the best part.

Traditionally you should eat paella directly out of the pan with friends gathered around. It goes great with sangria, but I prefer a cracking good pils.

SERVES 6

BEER NOTES

Try Peroni Nastro Azzurro, Pilsner Urquell, Red Angus Pilsener, James Squire Pilsener, Blue Tongue Traditional Pilsener, Matilda Bay Bohemian Pilsener, or one from your local micro-brewery

If you can't find Ronnie Dales sauce – and chances are you won't – use your favourite chilli sauce, piri piri or even just Tabasco. I find the lovely citrusy, hoppy character of an American pale ale works well with the char and caramelisation of the meat and the spiciness of the marinade. Some people like to first simmer the ribs in a saucepan of salted water for 20–30 minutes to cook out some of the fat and to help tenderise them. Give it a try and see what you prefer.

Beer rub for ribs

60 g (2 oz/⅓ cup) brown sugar
1 teaspoon ground oregano
2 teaspoons garlic powder
2 teaspoons Mexican chilli powder
1 teaspoon lemon pepper
2 teaspoons smoked paprika
2 teaspoons mustard powder
1 teaspoon sea salt

2 tablespoons good-quality olive oil
2 tablespoons apple cider vinegar
90 ml (3 fl oz) American-style pale ale – such as Arctic Fox, Feral Hop Hog, Stone & Wood Pacific Ale, Hargreaves Hill Pale or Sierra Nevada Pale Ale
1 teaspoon Ronnie Dales La Habanero chilli sauce
8 pork spare ribs, about 1 kg (2 lb 4 oz) in total

Put all the ingredients except the ribs in a glass bowl or jug and stir well to combine. Lay the ribs in a large baking dish in a single layer and pour the marinade over. Turn the ribs to make sure they are all well coated. Cover the dish with plastic wrap and leave in the fridge for a couple of hours, or even overnight.

Fire up the barbecue to high heat. Cook the ribs over direct heat for 10 minutes, basting them with the excess marinade in the baking dish each time you turn them. Turn the heat down to medium and continue to turn and baste – it should take about 15 minutes to cook them, depending on your barbecue and which way the wind is blowing.

Serve two ribs per person, with a green garden salad or coleslaw (see page 146), and some barbecued corn on the cob.

SERVES 4

For this recipe your barbecue must have a lid, as the first part of the cooking process involves slow-roasting by indirect heat. The second stage will be direct-heat grilling. I love to do these ribs on the barbecue because of the added smokiness that you can't get from cooking them slowly in the oven. You can buy American-style ribs in every supermarket and butcher shop now – just keep an eye out for good meaty ones, as sometimes the meat-to-bone ratio can be more skewed towards the bone. I love to buy my American-style ribs at Chinese butchers as they always leave lots of meat on the ribs.

Barbecued American-style pork ribs

3 spring onions (scallions), white part only,
    finely sliced
1 tablespoon sesame oil
2 garlic cloves, crushed
1 teaspoon dijon or wholegrain mustard
1 teaspoon chilli paste
3 tablespoons hoisin sauce

3 tablespoons mango chutney – I use
    hot mango chutney when I can find it
½ teaspoon sea salt
¼ teaspoon freshly ground black pepper
125 ml (4 fl oz/½ cup) Coopers Sparkling Ale
2 racks of American-style pork ribs,
    600–700 g (1 lb 5 oz–1 lb 9 oz) each

Combine all the ingredients except the ribs in a bowl and mix well. I then like to pop it in the microwave for about 30 seconds to warm the ingredients up, allowing them to combine thoroughly. This also encourages all the flavours to come out and mingle.

Cut each pork rack into three sections and place them in a deep baking tin or roasting tin that they will all fit into. Pour the marinade over the ribs and turn them, making sure that each portion is well coated. Cover and marinate for an hour or two.

Preheat your barbecue or Weber kettle barbecue to moderate, about 170°C (325°F). Put the tin of ribs in the barbecue, with heat on either side of the tin, but not under it. Close the lid and cook for 1½–2 hours, checking and turning every 30 minutes. Every barbecue is going to hold heat and cook differently, so just keep an eye on it. When the ribs pull away from the bone easily and the meat is juicy and tender, they are done.

Now take the ribs out of the tin and grill them directly over medium–high heat for about 10 minutes, turning and basting the ribs with the marinade from the tin. This will caramelise the outside of the ribs and give them a little char or 'bark', and keep the inside fork-tender. Remove from the heat, pile on a plate and eat.

My wife and I usually have a Greek salad with this dish. The recipe for that is in my first cookbook – *Mercurio's Menu*.

SERVES 2

BEER NOTES
A malt-driven ale is always good with this marinade

Quails slathered with hot and spicy barbecue sauce

6 quails
olive oil, for rubbing
185 ml (6 fl oz/¾ cup) hot and spicy barbecue
    sauce (see page 149)

COLESLAW
225 g (8 oz/3 cups) very finely sliced wombok
    (Chinese cabbage)
1 large carrot, grated
1 celery stalk, very finely julienned
185 g (6½ oz/¾ cup) whole-egg mayonnaise
1 tablespoon white wine vinegar
juice of ½ small lemon
1½ teaspoons caster (superfine) sugar

Put all the coleslaw ingredients in a big bowl, season to taste with sea salt and freshly ground black pepper and give them a good mix. Cover and refrigerate until required.

Preheat the barbecue grill to high.

Rinse each quail under cold water, then pat dry with paper towels. Turn one over so it lies breast side down and, using a pair of kitchen scissors, cut along one side of the backbone, from its bum to its neck. Then cut along the other side and remove the backbone. Turn the quail back over so that it is splayed out on your chopping board and, using the palm of your hand, press down firmly on the breast until it cracks. The quail will now lie flat on the chopping board. Repeat with the other quails.

Rub a little olive oil over the quails, then season both sides of each bird with sea salt and freshly ground black pepper. Put them skin side down on the barbecue grill and cook for 3 minutes, then turn them over and cook the other side for 3 minutes – you want to get a nice char on the birds, but not cook them through just yet.

Using a pastry brush, slather the barbecue sauce all over the birds, then turn them over and slather again. Reduce the heat of the barbecue to medium–low so you don't burn the birds, then cook them for another 10 minutes. This is my favourite part as I like to slather the birds, have a swig of beer, turn them over, slather and sip, etc – you get the picture. Continue to cook, baste and turn until the birds are done to your liking and have a lovely rich colour from the sauce, and a nice barbecue charred character – it's probably a total cooking time of 15 minutes. Some people like to serve their quail pink and I say good for them, but not for me as I like my game cooked through, although definitely not overcooked.

Pile the quails on a plate and serve with your coleslaw.

SERVES 4

Hot and spicy barbecue sauce

1 tablespoon olive oil

440 g (15½ oz) tin chopped tomatoes

95 g (3¼ oz/½ cup) soft brown sugar

375 ml (13 fl oz/1½ cups) stout

60 ml (2 fl oz/¼ cup) apple cider vinegar

2 tablespoons worcestershire sauce

1 tablespoon Wild Turkey or other bourbon

1½ teaspoons liquid smoke (available from barbecue stockists and specialist food stores)

1 star anise

1 cinnamon stick

2 teaspoons garlic powder

2 teaspoons onion powder

1 teaspoon cayenne pepper

2 teaspoons smoked paprika

1 teaspoon mustard powder

½ teaspoon ground ginger

½ teaspoon celery seeds

Heat the olive oil in a saucepan over medium–high heat. When the oil is hot, add the tomatoes and cook, stirring, for several minutes. Add the sugar, stout, vinegar, worcestershire sauce, bourbon and liquid smoke. Stir well and bring to the boil. Add the star anise and cinnamon stick, reduce the heat and simmer for 10 minutes. Stir in the remaining ingredients and simmer for another 20 minutes.

Discard the cinnamon stick and star anise and put the sauce in a blender. Process until smooth, then return the sauce to the pan and simmer for a final 10 minutes. Taste for seasoning and add sea salt and freshly ground black pepper as needed. The sauce should now be a thick pouring consistency – if you over-reduced it, add some more stout to loosen it up.

MAKES 375 ML (13 FL OZ/1½ CUPS)

BEER NOTES
Coopers Best Extra Stout is good for this sauce, as are Red Hill Brewery Imperial Stout, Moo Brew Imperial Stout or Lord Nelson Old Admiral

Taieri George is a strong (6.8 per cent) spicy ale from Emerson's Brewery in New Zealand. It is a unique beer with a beautiful spice character. This beer will be hard to find, but is well worth seeking out. If you can't find it, use a Scotch ale, Seven Sheds Kentish Ale or an imperial stout and flavour it with star anise, cinnamon, cloves and a little nutmeg.

Spiced ale-marinated duck breast

1 cinnamon stick
6 cloves
1 teaspoon ground ginger
½ teaspoon garlic powder
1 star anise
¾ teaspoon smoked paprika
1 teaspoon brown sugar
2 duck breasts, skin on
500 ml (17 fl oz/2 cups) Taieri George
1 tablespoon olive oil

FENNEL CAESAR SALAD
1 free-range egg
1 garlic clove, crushed
3–4 anchovy fillets
80 ml (2½ fl oz/⅓ cup) good-quality olive oil
25 g (1 oz/¼ cup) grated parmesan cheese
10 cos (romaine) lettuce leaves
1 baby fennel bulb, grated

Combine the spices and sugar in a bowl that will hold the duck breasts in one layer. Lightly score the duck skin in a diamond pattern, then turn the breasts in the spice mix to give them a bit of a coating. Lay them meat side down, then pour in the beer. Cover with plastic wrap and marinate in the fridge overnight, or for up to 3 days.

Heat the barbecue grill plate to high, then pour the olive oil onto it. When the oil begins to smoke, place the duck, skin side down, on the grill and cook for 5 minutes, being careful not to burn the skin. Turn and cook the other side for 2–3 minutes, then turn the heat down to medium and cook the duck to medium–rare, about 2 minutes, turning twice more. Remove from the heat and rest in a warm spot for a few minutes.

Meanwhile, make the salad. Using a mini food processor, blend the egg, garlic and anchovies together. Blend in a little olive oil, then keep adding more oil a little at a time until you have the consistency of pouring cream; you may not use all the olive oil, or you may need a little more. Add the cheese and blend again. Put the lettuce in a bowl, pour the dressing over – enough to dress the leaves but not drown them – then add the fennel and toss together. Divide the salad between two plates.

Slice the duck breasts at a slight angle and serve on top of the salad. Spicy beetroot chutney (see page 153) is nice with this dish.

SERVES 2

Wheat beer vinaigrette

3 tablespoons wit beer or Belgian wheat beer
125 ml (4 fl oz/½ cup) olive oil
3 tablespoons lemon juice

1 teaspoon balsamic vinegar
2 teaspoons wholegrain mustard
1 garlic clove, crushed

Put all the ingredients in a clean jar and add sea salt and freshly ground black pepper to taste. Put the lid on tightly and give the jar a good shake.

This dressing works very well with the roast potato, tomato and bean salad (see page 169) and my barbecued vegetable salad (see page 163). It's also great with a garden salad containing corn and beetroot – however I would use a sweeter version of this dressing by adding a tablespoon of honey to complement the corn and beetroot.

BEER NOTES
Try Hoegaarden Witbier, Feral White, Bright Brewery Razor Witbier, Wicked Elf Witbier or White Rabbit White Ale

Spicy beetroot chutney

2–3 medium beetroot (beets), about 550 g
    (1 lb 4 oz) total weight
1 tablespoon olive oil
1 onion, finely sliced
1 garlic clove, crushed
70 ml (2¼ fl oz) freshly squeezed orange juice
2 fresh bay leaves
125 ml (4 fl oz/½ cup) apple cider vinegar

250 ml (9 fl oz/1 cup) White Rabbit Dark Ale –
    you could also use Seven Sheds Kentish Ale,
    or even a porter such as Bright Brewery
    Staircase Porter
45 g (1½ oz/¼ cup) brown sugar
½ teaspoon chilli flakes, or 1 teaspoon if you
    like your chutney really hot
1 teaspoon smoked paprika

Preheat the oven to 200°C (400°F/Gas 6). Wrap each beetroot individually in foil and bake for 1 hour. Remove from the oven and leave until cool enough to handle. Unwrap the beetroot, then peel and remove the skin. Cut the bulbs into small dice.

Heat the olive oil in a deep saucepan over medium–high heat and fry the onion until softened. Add all the other ingredients except the beetroot and simmer for about 10 minutes.

Now add the beetroot and season with sea salt and freshly ground black pepper. Simmer for about 40 minutes, stirring occasionally, until most of the liquid has evaporated. Cool a little, then pour into sterilised jars (see note below).

MAKES TWO 500 G (1 LB 2 OZ) JARS

NOTE: To sterilise jars, first wash them and their lids in hot soapy water and rinse them well. Put the jars – and the lids if they're metal – in the oven at 120°C (235°F/Gas ½) for 30 minutes. If the lids are plastic, put them in a saucepan, cover them with water and boil them for 5 minutes.

Hot diggity dogs

4 good-quality fresh sausages, such as bratwurst, pork, chorizo or kransky
1–2 tablespoons olive oil
2 large onions, sliced
180 g (6 oz/1 cup) sauerkraut

330 ml (11¼ fl oz) bottle of American-style pale ale
4 long bread rolls
kick-arse hot beer mustard (see page 166)
tomato sauce (ketchup), to taste
125 g (4½ oz/1 cup) grated cheddar cheese

Preheat the barbecue grill to medium–high. Throw the sausages on and brown them on all sides, then reduce heat to medium and continue to cook and turn until done.

While the sausages are cooking, turn the hotplate heat to high and drizzle the hotplate with the olive oil. Throw on the onion and cook for about 5 minutes, stirring often. Reduce the heat to medium and cook the onion for another 15–20 minutes, stirring occasionally. When the onion is about done, add the sauerkraut and mix well to combine. Pour about one-third of the bottle of beer over the mixture – and drink the rest. Fry until the beer has cooked out, the sauerkraut is hot and the onion has caramelised.

Slice open a bread roll lengthways, then smother one side with the mustard and the other with tomato sauce. Plop a sausage in. Put a generous amount of the onion and sauerkraut mixture on top, and lastly sprinkle on some of the grated cheese. Make another three hot dogs like this.

Eat! Make sure you have some napkins on hand because the hot dogs are supposed to get messy!

MAKES 4

BEER NOTES
Good choices for this dish include Arctic Fox American Pale Ale, Hargreaves Hill Pale or Wicked Elf Pale Ale; you could also use Coopers Sparkling Ale or a stout

Sometimes when you are cooking you just have to make do with what you have available, even if it doesn't quite fit in with your idea of a dish. Don't be afraid to improvise when it comes to food – this salad is a case in point. I had thought to make a coleslaw to go with the skewers but the only place I could shop was at a little Vietnamese garden market. They had some beautiful fresh market produce but not one cabbage or carrot in sight! So I went with the flow, bought the freshest ingredients – in fact I picked them myself – and made this slaw-type salad. For me, part of what makes a good slaw is how finely shredded all the ingredients are, and the other part is the dressing.

Chicken satay with Vietnamese salad

1 teaspoon sea salt
¼ teaspoon ground white pepper
½ teaspoon ground lemon myrtle
3 skinless free-range chicken breasts

VIETNAMESE SALAD
1 bok choy (pak choy), trimmed
½ long Chinese radish
3 radishes
10 fresh mint leaves
1 pink grapefruit
185 g (6½ oz/¾ cup) good-quality mayonnaise
1 tablespoon white wine vinegar
1½ teaspoons caster (superfine) sugar
a small pinch of ground white pepper
40 g (1½ oz/¼ cup) cashews, lightly crushed
fresh coriander (cilantro) leaves, to garnish

SATAY SAUCE
1 tablespoon peanut oil
1 small onion, finely diced
1 garlic clove, finely sliced
1 teaspoon grated fresh ginger
1 long red chilli, finely sliced
80 ml (2½ fl oz/⅓ cup) coconut milk
125 ml (4 fl oz/½ cup) Coopers Original Pale Ale
160 g (5¾ oz/⅔ cup) crunchy peanut butter
3 teaspoons soy sauce
1 teaspoon sugar
juice of ½ lemon
1 tablespoon chopped fresh coriander (cilantro)

Soak some wooden skewers in water for an hour so they don't scorch when you put them on the barbecue.

In a bowl, combine the salt, pepper and lemon myrtle. Carefully cut each chicken breast into thin slices about 4 mm (⅙ inch) thick and 8–10 cm (3¼–4 inches) long. Thread each slice lengthways onto a skewer and season with the spice mix. Set aside until ready to cook. You can easily make these a day ahead – just cover them with plastic wrap and leave in the fridge.

To make the satay sauce, heat the oil in a saucepan over medium heat. Add the onion and cook, stirring, until translucent. Add the garlic, ginger and chilli and cook for about 5 minutes, stirring occasionally. Add the coconut milk, beer and peanut butter and stir or whisk until well combined. Stir in the soy sauce and the sugar, and finally the lemon juice and coriander. Spoon off any oil that rises to the top; if need be you can add a little water or beer to thin the sauce out.

To make the salad, very finely slice the bok choy stalks lengthways, then finely slice the leaves. Cut the Chinese radish into very fine julienne about 7.5 cm (3 inches) long. Finely julienne the other radishes, and finely slice the mint. Place them all in a large bowl. Cut the peel off the grapefruit, removing all the white pith and exposing the flesh. Working over a bowl to catch the juices, cut the fleshy segments from their membranes. Cut the segments into small cubes, then add half the grapefruit to the salad and mix thoroughly. Pour about 3 tablespoons of the reserved grapefruit juice into a bowl, then add the mayonnaise, vinegar, sugar, pepper and a pinch of sea salt and give it a good mix. Taste for seasoning and adjust as needed. Add most of the dressing to the salad and mix again, then add the rest if you think it needs it. Pile the salad in the middle of a large, flat serving plate, then garnish with the remaining grapefruit, cashews and some coriander leaves.

Cook the chicken skewers on a hot barbecue grill until done, 4–5 minutes each side. Arrange on a large plate and drizzle with some of the satay sauce. Serve the rest of the sauce in a bowl on the side, for extra dipping.

SERVES 4

BEER NOTES
You could also use a malt-driven English pale ale from English brewers such as Bass, Boddingtons, Fuller's or Samuel Smiths

Sweet marinated chook with ale and coriander

4 small red chillies, chopped
4 garlic cloves, crushed
4 tablespoons chopped fresh coriander (cilantro)
185 ml (6 fl oz/¾ cup) unsweetened pineapple juice

375 ml (13 fl oz) bottle of Coopers Sparkling Ale
2 tablespoons soy sauce
2 tablespoons tomato sauce (ketchup)
1 large free-range chicken, cut into quarters

Put all the ingredients except the chicken in a bowl. Add a pinch of sea salt, give it a good mix and taste – the marinade should be hot, spicy, sweet and salty. Let the marinade sit for 15 minutes so that the flavours bond with each other.

With a sharp knife, slash the chicken breasts and legs – but not too deeply – to allow the marinade to get into the meat. Put the chicken in a roasting tin or a baking dish so that the pieces fit snugly, then pour the marinade over them. Turn the chicken pieces over a few times to coat them all over. Leave them skin side down and spoon some of the marinade over the bits that are sticking up. Cover with plastic wrap and leave for 1 hour at room temperature, or up to 24 hours in the fridge.

Preheat your barbecue grill to high, then put the chicken, skin side down, on the grill. Cook for about 5 minutes, then turn the chicken pieces over and cook for another 5 minutes or so. You want to get good colour on the meat, but not burn it. Turn the heat down to medium and cook for about 30 minutes, turning the pieces every 8 minutes or so, and basting the chicken with the marinade every time. (I move my chicken around the barbecue, depending on where the hot spots are, and I turn the breasts and the legs and baste them often to ensure even cooking. Doing this and cooking at a low temperature help to keep the meat moist.)

Check the joints of the leg to see if the chicken is done – they should move quite freely and there shouldn't be any blood or red flesh. The juices should also run clear if you poke the chicken with a barbecue fork. If there are signs of blood in the juice or in the joints, cook the chicken a bit longer.

Put the chicken on a plate and cover with foil to rest for 5 minutes before serving. Serve with a rice salad.

SERVES 4

BEER NOTES

You can try a few different beers with this dish – say a Lord Nelson Three Sheets, Seven Sheds Kentish Ale or Moo Brew Dark Ale – just be sure to use a malt-driven ale, as the malt will caramelise during the grilling and add a lovely sweetness to the chicken

If you've never cooked this dish, it's high time you did – it is truly delicious and remarkably simple, although you'll need a barbecue with a lid. You may think your beer choices are slightly limited as this recipe requires an actual can. However, if you think outside the square you can use any beer you want: just buy a can of beer and if the beer is not to your liking, tip it down the sink and then fill the empty can with the beer of your choice!

Beer can chicken

1.8 kg (4 lb) free-range chicken
1 can of beer – I used an English ale called
    Boddingtons; James Squire Golden Ale
      comes in a can and is also a good choice
½ lemon, cut into four wedges
1 garlic clove, bruised

BASTING MIXTURE
50 g (1¾ oz) butter, softened
1 teaspoon sea salt
¼ teaspoon freshly ground black pepper
1 teaspoon sweet paprika
2 garlic cloves, crushed

Preheat your barbecue or Weber kettle barbecue for indirect roasting. Rinse the chicken under cold water, then pat dry with paper towels.

If you're using a tall can of one of the English ales that have a widget in the can – such as Boddingtons, Guinness or Kilkenny – pour the beer into a glass and drink one-third of the beer. Next, cut the top one-third of the can away (otherwise the chicken may not fit under your barbecue lid!) and discard the plastic widget. If you're using an ordinary can of beer, pour off or drink one-third of the beer. Now place three lemon wedges in the can, along with the garlic clove. (You could also add some herbs or a chilli if you want.) Pick the chicken up and carefully impale it on the beer can – it should sit snugly on the can, with its legs keeping it balanced. Make sure the wings are tucked in and not hanging free.

Put the basting ingredients in a bowl and mix together well. Using a pastry brush, liberally baste the chicken with the mixture. Put the chicken on the barbecue or in the Weber, close the lid and cook for 30 minutes. Baste the chook liberally, close the lid, then cook for another 30 minutes. Check and baste again – the chicken should be cooked after 1–1¼ hours. If you pierce the chook in the breast or leg joint and the juices run clear, the chook is cooked.

Carefully take the chicken off the can – the beer in the can is very hot! Pull the chicken apart to serve, or cut it into quarters. Eat it with a green salad – or even better, my barbecued vegetable salad (see opposite page).

SERVES 4

Barbecued vegetable salad

2 large spring onions (scallions)
1 yellow capsicum (pepper)
1 red capsicum (pepper)
1 large zucchini (courgette)
1 eggplant (aubergine)
1 radicchio

250 g (9 oz) haloumi cheese
3–4 tablespoons plain (all-purpose) flour
125 ml (4 fl oz/½ cup) olive oil, approximately
8 large cherry tomatoes, halved
wheat beer vinaigrette (see page 151), for dressing

Preheat your barbecue hotplate to high.

Meanwhile, trim the spring onions, discard the top green third, then cut them in half and set aside. Cut two sides off each capsicum, then slice these into strips and set aside. (The remainder can be saved for another day.) Trim the zucchini, cut it in half lengthways, then cut each half into three wedges lengthways. Cut the bottom 3 cm (1¼ inches) off the fat end of the eggplant and save it for another time. Cut four discs about 1 cm (½ inch) thick from what's left of the eggplant, then cut each slice in half and set aside. Peel 12 good leaves from the radicchio and set aside; the rest can be saved for another time.

Cut the haloumi into slabs 8 mm (⅜ inch) thick. Put the flour, a pinch of sea salt and a few grinds of black pepper into a clean plastic bag. Add the haloumi and shake the bag so that the cheese is coated with the seasoned flour. Remove the haloumi, shaking off the excess flour, then set aside.

Pour about 3 tablespoons of the olive oil onto the hotplate and when hot, add the haloumi. Put the spring onion, capsicum, zucchini and eggplant pieces onto the hotplate, making sure they are in some oil, especially the eggplant. Cook the vegies, turning often so you get good colour on them. When the haloumi is golden brown on both sides, take it off the hotplate and put the tomatoes on. Keep turning the vegies and adding a little more oil to the eggplant if needed. You don't want the vegies to become soggy, nor do you want to overcook them – you are after a really lovely charred colour and caramelised flavour.

As the different vegetables are cooked, take them off the barbecue and put them in a large salad bowl. Right when you are about to take off the last vegies, throw the radicchio leaves on the hotplate for about 30 seconds, just so they wilt.

Put all the vegies and the haloumi in the salad bowl. Dress with the wheat beer vinaigrette and toss to combine.

SERVES 4–6

What makes a great steak sandwich? First and foremost the steak itself: it needs to be the right thickness – not too thick and not too thin. Second, you need the right cut of steak, with the perfect ratio of fat to meat so it's tender, full of flavour and a joy to eat. And third, eatability – there's nothing worse than a steak sandwich that you can't get your mouth around. You need to be able to pick it up and bite into it without it falling apart or having its contents falling through your fingers. So with that in mind my steak sandwich starts with a slice of beautiful wagyu beef, with a marbling rating of 8–9. Add some good sourdough bread, a free-range egg, something green with a bit of bite, something crisp and spicy, some mayo, homemade chutney and a little cheese and you can't go wrong!

Wagyu steak sandwich

2 garlic cloves, crushed
3 tablespoons olive oil
2 sourdough slices, cut on the diagonal
1 free-range egg
1 slice wagyu scotch fillet, 5 mm (¼ inch) thick
1 teaspoon blue cheese

1–2 tablespoons good-quality whole-egg
 mayonnaise
2 radishes, grated
1 handful rocket (arugula)
spicy beetroot chutney (see page 153)

Put the garlic in a small bowl with the olive oil and set aside to let the flavours combine. Preheat your barbecue grill to medium–high.

Brush the bread on both sides with the olive oil mixture, then toast one side on the grill. When those lovely dark grill lines appear, turn and toast the other side. (Everything can be cooked at the same time, although the toast probably takes longest so put that on first, then the egg, and lastly the steak.) Cook the egg on the hotplate, brushed with a little olive oil to stop it sticking. Grill the steak to your liking – I like mine medium-rare, which is probably a couple of minutes on each side. Carefully turn the egg just before you put it on the sandwich so you seal the top side but don't break the yolk, as one of the pleasures of a good steak sandwich is when the egg breaks as you bite into it and the yolk runs down your arm.

When the bread is ready, spread the blue cheese on one piece and then slather some mayo over it. Put the steak on this, followed by some grated radish, the unbroken egg and then the rocket. On the other piece of bread, liberally spread some beetroot chutney, then put it on top of the sandwich. Eat! Extravagant? Yes. Delicious? Yes. The best steak sandwich ever? – I have heard some say it is.

MAKES 1

I like to add an egg yolk to this mustard – it silkens the texture but shortens the shelf life, so if you want the mustard to last for while, leave out the yolk.

Kick-arse hot beer mustard

2 teaspoons black mustard seeds
½ teaspoon celery seeds
6 tablespoons Keen's or other mustard powder
1 teaspoon garlic powder
1 teaspoon onion powder
1 teaspoon cayenne pepper
½ teaspoon ground turmeric

½ teaspoon sea salt
2 tablespoons soft brown sugar
1 tablespoon apple cider vinegar
90 ml (3 fl oz) Coopers Sparkling Ale, Stone & Wood Pacific Ale or Wicked Elf Pale Ale
1 egg yolk – free-range of course (optional)

Using a mortar and pestle, grind the mustard seeds and celery seeds to a powder. Tip the powder into a glass bowl and add the mustard powder, spices, salt and sugar. Mix well.

Add the vinegar and beer and whisk it as smooth as you can. If you have a hand-held blender use that for a minute or two, otherwise put the mixture in a blender and blend it for a minute or two. Return the mixture to the bowl and whisk in the egg yolk, if using.

Place the bowl over a saucepan of barely simmering water, making sure the bowl fits snugly but does not come in contact with the water. Whisk the mustard for about 3 minutes – it will thicken slightly and become creamy smooth.

Put the mustard in a sterilised jar (see note on page 153) and keep it in the fridge.

MAKES 170 ML (5½ FL OZ/⅔ CUP)

I love this salad because of its simplicity and because it goes so well with anything you cook on the barbecue. The salty, spicy crunch from the potatoes, the sweetness of the tomato, the bite from the onion, the pepper from the coriander and the earthiness of the beans all combine to complement those wonderful smoky characters you get from cooking meat over flames or hot coals. Yum!

Roast potato, tomato and bean salad

3 potatoes, peeled
1–2 tablespoons olive oil
a pinch of chilli powder (optional)
300 g (10½ oz) green beans, topped and tailed
½ red onion, halved and finely sliced
10 cherry tomatoes, quartered

20 g (¾ oz/⅓ cup) chopped fresh coriander (cilantro)
3–4 tablespoons wheat beer vinaigrette (see page 151)

Preheat the oven to 200°C (400°F/Gas 6).

Cut the potatoes in half lengthways, cut each half into thirds, then cut across those into quarters – you should now have about 12 potato squares from each half. The idea is to have the potato squares roughly the same size, but don't worry if they aren't as the smaller squares crisp up beautifully and are usually the ones we fight over in my house!

Put the potatoes on a baking tray, drizzle with the olive oil and sprinkle with a little sea salt and some chilli powder, if using. Give them a good toss and roast for about 30 minutes, or until the potatoes are crisp and brown on the outside, and soft and fluffy in the middle. Remove from the oven and leave to cool.

Blanch the beans in some boiling salted water for 2–3 minutes, or put them in a microwave dish with a little water and zap them for 1–2 minutes – you still want some 'bite' in the beans, so don't overcook them. Drain the beans and allow to cool.

Put the beans in a salad bowl with the onion, tomato and coriander. When the potatoes are lukewarm, add those also. Dress the salad with the wheat beer vinaigrette and serve straight away, so the potatoes don't become soggy.

SERVES 4

Beer for dessert

I love to watch people's faces when I describe some of my beer desserts to them. First there is a look of disbelief, followed by surprise, shock, disgust, fear, concern, curiosity, daring or interest – and then finally a smile touches their eyes. It quickly spreads across their face as the idea that beer, cream, sugar, fruit, eggs, coffee, flour and chocolate might actually work together in some strange and unfathomable way. Then the slightly naughty and guilty admission that they would love to try it escapes their lips, quickly followed by the statement that their mouth is now watering at the thought of it. Yes, the idea of beer in dessert is somewhat of a stretch of the imagination for most normal people, but that prompts the question – what really is normal? Well, once you start making beer desserts I guarantee 'normal' will never be normal ever again – nor will dessert for that matter.

Dark lagers are lovely beers to cook with as they can add a nutty or even woody character to your dish, without contributing much sweetness.

Bread and butter pudding

4 free-range eggs
2 free-range egg yolks
125 g (4½ oz) caster (superfine) sugar
400 ml (14 fl oz) whipping cream
200 ml (7 fl oz) dark lager
1 teaspoon vanilla extract

14 slices wholegrain organic bread,
    crusts removed
60 g (2¼ oz) unsalted butter, melted,
    plus extra for greasing
100 g (3½ oz/¾ cup) frozen blueberries

Preheat the oven to 170°C (325°F/Gas 3).

Beat the eggs, egg yolks and sugar in a bowl until well combined. Pour the cream, beer and vanilla into a separate bowl and mix together well, then add the egg mixture and mix again until well combined. Set aside.

Using a pastry brush, brush both sides of the bread slices with the melted butter. Cut each slice in half on the diagonal, so you end up with two triangles per slice. Grease a 27 x 18 cm (10¾ x 7 inch) baking dish with a little butter and then layer the bread inside it, overlapping each slice. (Depending on the size of your dish, you may or may not use all the bread.) Once all the bread is layered, scatter the blueberries over, tucking them down in between each slice of bread and over the top. Pour the custard mixture over the bread and let it settle. You might not use all the mixture at first, but once the bread has soaked up the liquid you will be able to pour in the rest. Let the pudding sit for 15 minutes.

Line a large roasting tin with several layers of paper towel. Place the pudding dish on the paper towels and pour enough boiling water into the roasting tin to reach halfway up the sides of the pudding dish. Cover with foil and bake for 25 minutes.

Remove the foil and bake for 15–20 minutes more, until the top is golden brown and the pudding is set. (If the eggs in the custard curdle, it means you have cooked the pudding on too high a heat. This won't affect the flavour, but next time reduce the heat a little.)

Remove the pudding from the roasting tin. Allow to cool a little before serving.

SERVES 8

BEER NOTES
I used Coldstream Brewery Dark Lager; other versions include Matilda Bay Dogbolter Dark Lager or Samuel Adams Black Lager

Kriek lambic is made with morello cherries, but other fruit lambic beers are also made using blackcurrants (cassis) or raspberries (framboise). So if you like you could use the corresponding beer and fruit, so raspberries with the framboise or blackcurrants with the cassis. Timmermans also makes a lambic called Fruits of the World, which is made with a mixture of fruits, so you could use that with a selection of fruit. In every case, frozen fruit can be used when fresh is not available. You can also use bottled morello cherries, which are terrific, or even a mix of half locally grown fresh cherries and half bottled morello cherries.

Morello kriek clafoutis

melted unsalted butter, for greasing,
    plus 1 tablespoon melted butter, extra
40 g (1½ oz/¼ cup) self-raising flour
25 g (1 oz/¼ cup) ground almonds
4 free-range eggs
45 g (1½ oz/¼ cup) brown sugar
150 ml (7 fl oz) milk

150 ml (5 fl oz) whipping cream
100 ml (3½ fl oz) kriek lambic
1 tablespoon port
600 g (1 lb 5 oz) pitted fresh morello cherries
    (see note above)
finely grated zest of 1 lemon
finely grated zest of 1 orange

Preheat the oven to 180°C (350°F/Gas 4). Brush a deep, 20 cm (8 inch) ovenproof dish with melted butter. (The bottom of a tagine is the ideal size for this dish.)

Sift the flour and a pinch of sea salt into a bowl, then mix the ground almonds through. In a separate bowl, whisk the eggs, sugar, milk, cream, beer and port together. Gradually incorporate the egg mixture into the flour mixture, whisking all the time until you finally have a smooth, liquid batter. Set this aside.

If you have extra-large cherries cut them in half, or if you are using frozen or bottled cherries leave them whole. Arrange them in the baking dish – the bottom of the dish should be completely covered. Mix the lemon and orange zest into the extra tablespoon of melted butter, then whisk it into the batter. Carefully pour the batter over the cherries.

Bake for about 35 minutes – the clafoutis should be firm to the touch and browned on top, but it should also wobble in a firm way. Serve with good-quality ice cream, yoghurt or some whipped cream.

SERVES 8

BEER NOTES
Timmermans,
Lindeman's,
Belle-Vue Brewery,
Cantillon Brewery
and Boon make
lambic beers

Birramisu

3 free-range eggs, separated
90 g (3¼ oz) caster (superfine) sugar
250 ml (9 fl oz/1 cup) whipping cream
250 g (9 oz) mascarpone cheese
60 ml (2 fl oz/¼ cup) Kahlua or other
   coffee-flavoured liqueur
500 ml (17 fl oz/2 cups) stout

60 ml (2 fl oz/¼ cup) espresso coffee – if you
   don't have an espresso machine at home,
   ask your local coffee shop to make you
   a couple of espressos to go
500 g (1 lb 2 oz) savoiardi (lady finger) biscuits,
   about 24
100 g (3½ oz) dark chocolate (70% cocoa), grated

Put the egg yolks and sugar in a bowl and beat using a cake mixer or electric beaters on moderate speed for about 10 minutes, or until pale and thick. Meanwhile, whip the cream in a separate bowl, being careful not to overbeat it. In another bowl, whisk the egg whites until stiff peaks form.

When the egg yolk and sugar are done, add the mascarpone and beat gently with electric beaters until well combined. Remove the bowl from the mixer and, using a spatula, gently fold the whipped cream through and add the Kahlua, mixing well. Now fold the beaten egg white through. Pour the stout and espresso into a flat dish.

You can make this tiramisu in individual portions, or as one big dessert in a large rectangular baking dish. I make mine in a lasagne dish measuring about 27 x 18 x 5 cm (10¾ x 7 x 2 inches). Spread a thin layer of the mascarpone mixture on the bottom of the dish. Dip a savoiardi biscuit in the stout and coffee mixture for about 4 seconds per side – you don't want the biscuit to become soggy. Place it on top of the mascarpone mixture at one end of the dish. Repeat the process, laying the biscuits side by side until you have a layer covering the bottom of the dish.

Spoon a thick layer of the mascarpone mixture over the biscuits, then sprinkle half the grated chocolate over the top. Repeat the savoiardi layer, gently pressing them onto the mixture underneath. Spread the remaining mascarpone mixture over the top and finish by sprinkling the last of the grated chocolate over.

Cover with plastic wrap and refrigerate for several hours before serving.

SERVES 8–10

BEER NOTES
You could use Coopers Best Extra Stout, Mountain Goat Surefoot Stout, Moo Brew Imperial Stout, Nail Brewing Company Nail Stout, Southwark Old Stout, Otway Estate Prickly Moses Stout or Lord Nelson Old Admiral

This ice cream is great with the caramelised beer nanas on page 184!

Wheat beer ice cream

250 ml (9 fl oz/1 cup) Belgian-style wheat beer –
   try Hoegaarden Witbier, Feral White, Holgate
   White Ale, Wicked Elf Witbier, Bright Brewery
   Razor Witbier, Otway Estate Prickly Moses
   Wheat Beer or White Rabbit White Ale

125 ml (4 fl oz/½ cup) milk
165 g (5¾ oz/¾ cup) caster (superfine) sugar
1 free-range egg, beaten
500 ml (17 fl oz/2 cups) whipping cream

Put the beer in a saucepan over medium–high heat and reduce it to 80 ml (2½ fl oz/ ⅓ cup). Add the milk, sugar, egg and cream and heat gently, stirring until all the sugar has dissolved. Transfer the custard to a bowl and place in the fridge or freezer to chill.

Pour the custard into an ice-cream machine and churn according to the manufacturer's instructions. Serve immediately, or place in a container, cover and freeze until needed.

Alternatively, pour the custard into a shallow tray and place in the freezer. Mash it with a fork once it has started to freeze, as this will break up the ice crystals. Repeat this process two or three more times, until the ice cream is smooth but set. Cover with a tight-fitting lid and freeze until required.

MAKES 1 LITRE (35 FL OZ/4 CUPS)

Very sweet, very delicious and very, very simple!

Caramelised beer nanas

100 g (3½ oz/½ cup) brown sugar
60 ml (2 fl oz/¼ cup) Belgian-style wheat ale
2 bananas, halved lengthways

wheat beer ice cream (see page 180),
   to serve
chopped fresh mint, to garnish

Put the sugar and beer in a non-stick frying pan over medium–high heat and bring to the boil, stirring to dissolve the sugar. Once the mixture has become liquid, do not stir it anymore.

Turn the heat down and simmer gently for 20–30 minutes. When the caramel has reduced by about two-thirds, add the banana. Cook on one side for 3 minutes, then turn and cook on the other side for another 3 minutes. (Don't overcook the banana – you don't want it to go soggy.)

Put a generous scoop of ice cream in two bowls and drape two banana halves over the top. Garnish with mint and enjoy.

SERVES 2

BEER NOTES
Suitable ales include Hoegaarden Original White Ale, Otway Estate Prickly Moses Wheat Beer, White Rabbit White Ale, or a German-style wheat beer such as Schofferhofer Hefeweizen or Moo Brew Hefeweizen

Framboise poached pears with sabayon

4 beurre bosc pears
500 ml (17 fl oz/2 cups) framboise lambic beer –
    made by Timmermans, Lindeman's, Boon,
    Belle-Vue Brewery or Cantillon Brewery
110 g (3¾ oz/½ cup) caster (superfine) sugar
1 cinnamon stick
2 star anise
6 cloves
1 lemon peel strip, white pith removed

SABAYON

3 free-range egg yolks
75 g (2½ oz/⅓ cup) caster (superfine) sugar
125 ml (4 fl oz/½ cup) saison ale, such as Saison
    Dupont from Belgium, or one from Temple
    Brewing Company, Bridge Road Brewers
    or Otway Estate Prickly Moses Saison

Peel the pears, leaving the stems intact. Cut a very small amount off the bottom of each one so that it will sit upright without falling over.

Put the framboise, sugar, cinnamon stick, star anise, cloves and lemon peel in a large saucepan and add 200 ml (7 fl oz) water. Place over medium heat and stir until the sugar has dissolved. Turn the heat up so the poaching liquid is just boiling, then put the pears in so they are standing up. When the liquid begins to simmer again, adjust the heat so that the simmer is very, very gentle. Cover the pan with a lid or foil and cook the pears for about 1 hour. You want the pears to be soft but not soggy, so check them after 50 minutes – at this stage you can lie the pears down on their side, cook them for 10 minutes, then check again and turn them over.

Remove the pears using a slotted spoon, or carefully pick them up by the stem and put them in a bowl. Cover to keep them warm. Remove the solids from the syrup, then bring the syrup to the boil and reduce by half. Set aside and keep warm.

To make the sabayon sauce, fill a medium-sized saucepan one-quarter full of boiling water and put it over a gentle heat so that the water is barely simmering. Put the egg yolks and sugar in a glass bowl that fits snugly on top of the saucepan, but doesn't come in contact with the water. Leaving it off the heat, whisk until the egg yolks and sugar are well combined and thick.

Place the bowl on top of the saucepan and continue to whisk for 5 minutes, until the sauce thickens and doubles in size. Now add the beer, a little at a time, whisking all the time. Keep whisking for 10 minutes, or until the sauce has at least doubled in size, is glossy, smooth and thick enough to leave a trail when you scoop your whisk through it. This sauce needs to be served immediately – if it goes cold it will collapse.

Pour the syrup into four wide serving bowls and place a pear upright in the middle of each bowl. Spoon the warm sabayon over the pears and serve.

MAKES 4

Leffe crème caramel

125 ml (4 fl oz/½ cup) Belgian ale –
   Leffe Radieuse 8.5% is ideal
220 g (7¾ oz/1 cup) caster (superfine) sugar
310 ml (10¾ fl oz/1¼ cups) milk
300 ml (10½ fl oz/1¼ cups) whipping cream

3 free-range eggs
3 free-range egg yolks
45 g (1½ oz/¼ cup) brown sugar
2 tablespoons golden syrup (or use maple syrup,
   treacle or molasses)

Preheat the oven to 180°C (350°F/Gas 4).

Put the beer and caster sugar in a saucepan over medium heat and stir until the sugar has dissolved. Do not stir the mixture again once the sugar has dissolved or it will crystallise and won't form a caramel. Turn the heat up and let the syrup come to the boil, then adjust the heat so the syrup simmers but doesn't froth up over the top of the saucepan. Continue to cook and watch closely until the caramel turns a nice golden colour. Instead of stirring you can give the saucepan a little shake to make sure the caramel cooks evenly. Once it reaches the correct colour, remove from the heat and pour into a jug with a spout for easy pouring.

Divide the caramel evenly among eight 125 ml (4 fl oz/½ cup) ramekins, and give the mixture a swirl to coat the bottom of each ramekin evenly. Place in the fridge until needed, by which time the caramel should have set firm.

Combine the milk and cream in a saucepan over medium heat. Bring to a simmer – do not allow the mixture to boil – then remove from the heat.

Mix the eggs, egg yolks, brown sugar and golden syrup in a large heatproof bowl until well combined. Gradually whisk in the milk and cream mixture, then carefully ladle the mixture on top of the caramel in the ramekins.

Line a large roasting tin with several layers of paper towel. Place the ramekins on the paper towels and pour enough boiling water into the roasting tin to reach halfway up the side of the ramekins. Cover the roasting tin with foil and bake for 40 minutes, or until the custard has just set. Remove the ramekins from the roasting tin and allow to cool, before covering them with plastic wrap and putting them in the fridge. It is best to leave them for several hours or even overnight prior to serving.

To serve, dip the bottom of each ramekin in hot water, then run a flat-bladed knife around the inside edge of the ramekins. Position a plate over the top, then quickly turn the ramekin and plate over, so the plate is sitting on the work surface and the ramekin is sitting upside down on the plate. Tap the ramekin, then lift it up, leaving the custard sitting beautifully in the middle of the plate, with the beer caramel surrounding it.

MAKES 8

Sweet blintz with orange beer syrup

CREPES

150 g (5½ oz/1 cup) plain (all-purpose) flour
1 tablespoon caster (superfine) sugar
125 ml (4 fl oz/½ cup) milk
125 ml (4 fl oz/½ cup) Belgian ale
2 free-range eggs
a pinch of sea salt
1–2 teaspoons unsalted butter, for pan-frying

ORANGE BEER SYRUP

125 ml (4 fl oz/½ cup) orange juice
125 ml (4 fl oz/½ cup) mandarin juice
250 ml (9 fl oz/1 cup) La Chouffe or
    Hoegaarden Grand Cru
3 tablespoons caster (superfine) sugar

FILLING

350 g (12 oz/1½ cups) ricotta cheese
200 g (7 oz) cream cheese, softened
2 free-range egg yolks
60 g (2¼ oz/¼ cup) caster (superfine) sugar
2 teaspoons grated orange zest
2 teaspoons grated mandarin zest
2 teaspoons grated lemon zest

TO FINISH

2 heaped tablespoons unsalted butter, melted
1 tablespoon caster (superfine) sugar

Preheat the oven to 180°C (350°F/Gas 4) and line a baking tray with baking paper.

Whisk all the crepe ingredients (except the butter) in a bowl until smooth. Set aside to rest while you make the syrup and filling.

To make the orange beer syrup, combine all the ingredients in a saucepan over medium heat and cook until reduced by half. Set aside and keep warm.

Mix the filling ingredients in a bowl using electric beaters until well combined.

Heat a little butter in a non-stick frying pan over medium–high heat. When the butter foams, add a ladleful of the crepe mixture, swirling it around the pan to give a 12–14 cm (4½–5½ inch) diameter. You want the crepes to be quite thin, so add a little more milk and beer to the batter if you need to. Cook until little bubbles appear on the top, then use a spatula to flip the crepe over. Cook the other side, then remove from the pan and set aside. Repeat to make 12 crepes.

Lay a crepe out on the bench and spoon 2 tablespoons of the filling in the middle. Fold the crepe into a square parcel by folding each side over the filling, then patting the crepe down so it flattens a little. Place on the baking tray, folded side down, and repeat until all the crepes are used up. Finish the crepes by brushing the tops with the melted butter and sprinkling with the caster sugar. Bake for 15 minutes to heat the crepes through and to glaze them with the butter–sugar coating.

Remove the crepes from the oven, place two crepes on each plate and pour some syrup over them. Enjoy.

SERVES 6

BEER NOTES
For the crepes, try La Chouffe or Hoegaarden Grand Cru – lovely big Belgian ales – or the Biere de Garde from the Bridge Road Brewers Chevalier range, or Prickly Moses Reserve De Otway

Hops impart flavour and bitterness to beer. It is important for this recipe to buy a hop variety that will add a lovely floral citrusy character to the panna cotta without too much bitterness. I would suggest using Goldings, Saaz, Fuggles or Willamette. You can buy hops from your local home-brew shop in small packets, or if you have a friend who is into home brewing you could ask them to give you some hops. Just make sure you ask for a low-bitterness hop or your panna cotta may end up very bitter – something I quite like but my wife doesn't!

Hop panna cotta with a grapefruit and orange salad

7 g (⅙ oz) fresh hops flowers or hop plugs,
    or 5 g (⅛ oz) hop pellets
250 ml (9 fl oz/1 cup) milk, plus a little extra
4 teaspoons powdered gelatine, or 4–6 Gelita
    Titanium gelatine leaves
750 ml (26 fl oz/3 cups) whipping cream

125 g (4½ oz) caster (superfine) sugar
½ vanilla bean, split in half lengthways
1 pink grapefruit
1 navel orange

Put the hops in a muslin (cheesecloth) bag (or the cut-off foot from a new pair of pantyhose) and tie the end off. Put the 250 ml (9 fl oz/1 cup) milk in a saucepan and gently warm but do not boil it. When the milk is hot, turn off the heat and add the hops. Leave to steep for about 10 minutes.

Remove the hops bag and squeeze as much of the milk back into the saucepan as you can. Pour the milk into a jug, then top it back up to 250 ml (9 fl oz/1 cup) with more milk. The milk will be quite bitter – some might say unpleasant – but the cream and the sugar will balance that out.

If you're using powdered gelatine, pour 80 ml (2½ fl oz/⅓ cup) of the cream into a small bowl and sprinkle the gelatine in an even layer over the top. Leave it to go spongy. Pour the remaining cream and sugar into a saucepan.

If you're using gelatine leaves, put them in cold water and soak for about 7 minutes. Squeeze out the water and add the leaves to the hot cream mixture in the next step.

Scrape out the seeds from the vanilla bean and add them to the cream mixture with the vanilla bean. Bring to the boil, then take off the heat, remove the vanilla bean and stir in the hops milk. Add the softened gelatine and gently stir until dissolved, being careful not to create air bubbles on the surface. Pour the mixture into moulds or glasses and refrigerate for 3 hours, or until set – overnight is best.

Working over a bowl to catch the juice, peel and segment the grapefruit and the orange so all you have is the flesh of each fruit. Cut the flesh into small pieces and place in the bowl with the collected juice.

You can serve the panna cotta either in the glasses they were set in, or turned out of the ramekin onto a plate, each garnished with a teaspoon or two of the citrus salad and reserved juice.

I love this dish but it can be a little bitter for some people, so as an alternative you could serve it with some poached stone fruit to give it a sweeter edge.

MAKES 8–10

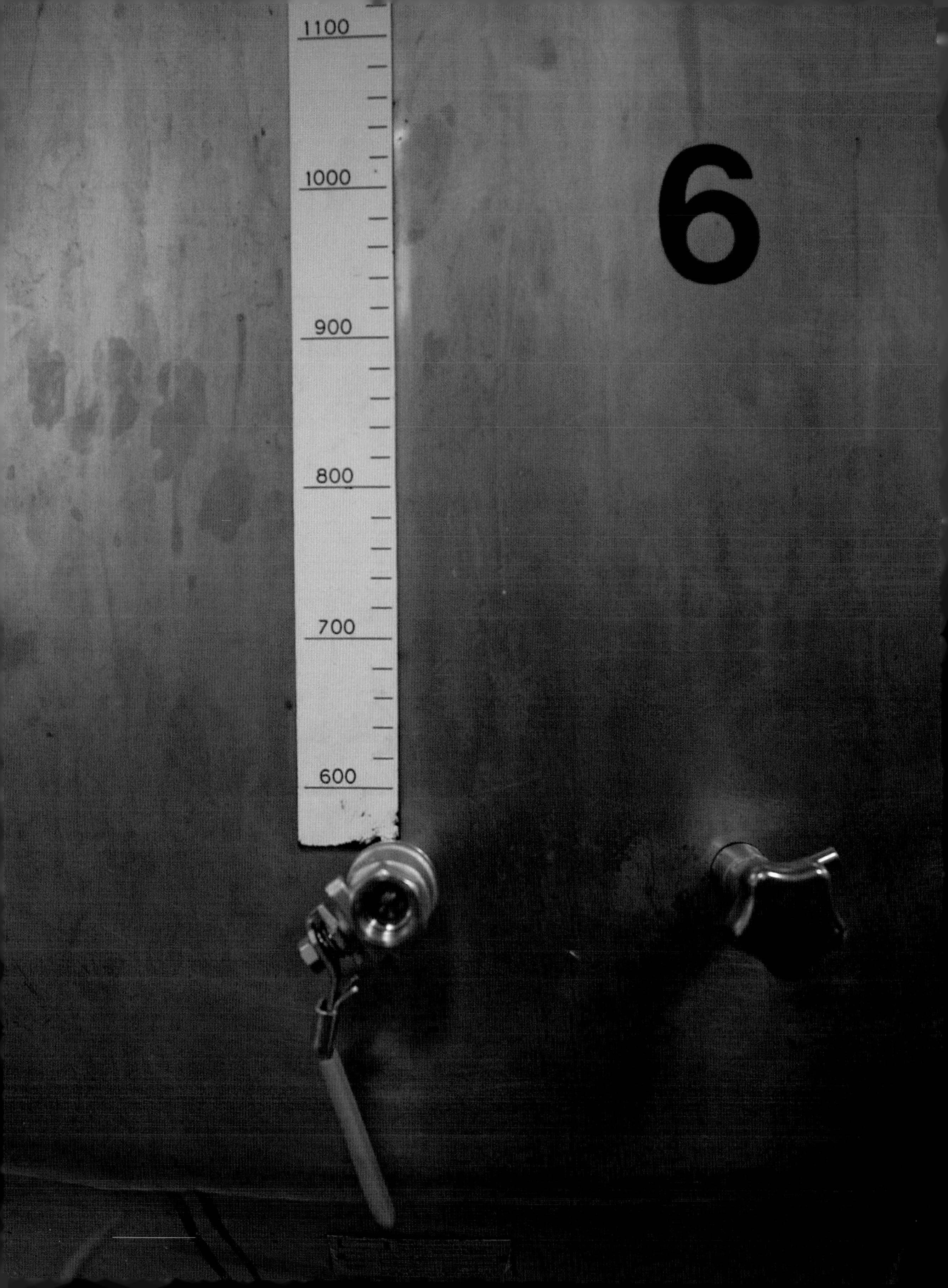
1100
1000
900
800
700
600
6

You can use any hot chilli you want for this ice cream, from the small red Thai bird's eye chilli to jalapeño to the very hot habanero – or, if you're game, a bhut jolokia, which is the hottest chilli in the world. I once used a chilli called fatali, which had a rich, fruity, almost mango-like aroma and flavour and was also very hot! Unfortunately I have never seen them in a store. You can also use whatever chocolate you desire – milk chocolate will give a more creamy chocolate character than a rich, dark chocolate. Lastly, I know some people like to reduce their stout or porter by up to two-thirds before adding it to the ice cream. My experience of reducing dark, bitter beer is that it becomes quite acrid and unpalatable, and you then have to add a lot of other sugars and flavours to balance it out; also you lose all those lovely malty flavours that make the ice cream special. So I don't recommend doing it here.

Chocolate chilli ice cream

125 ml (4 fl oz/½ cup) milk
165 g (5¾ oz/¾ cup) caster (superfine) sugar
1 free-range egg, beaten
500 ml (17 fl oz/2 cups) whipping cream
1 jalapeño chilli, halved, with seeds – or if you
     want to live dangerously use half a habanero

125 ml (4 fl oz/½ cup) stout, such as Guinness or
     Mountain Goat Surefoot Stout
100 g (3½ oz) milk chocolate, grated

Put all the ingredients except the chocolate in a saucepan and heat gently, stirring until all the sugar has dissolved and the egg is well combined. When the mixture is quite warm – do not let it boil or simmer – add the chocolate and stir constantly while it melts. You will find that the chocolate remains slightly grainy, so you get tiny little specks floating in the mixture. Once it has melted, remove the mixture from the heat and stir for 5–8 minutes to encourage the chilli to release its heat. When you are happy with the level of chilli heat, discard the chilli.

Put the mixture in a clean bowl and chill in the fridge or freezer until very cold. Pour into an ice-cream machine and churn until you get the desired consistency. Put the ice cream in a container with a lid and keep in the freezer until needed.

Alternatively, pour the custard into a shallow tray and place it in the freezer. Beat it vigorously once it has started to freeze, as this will break up the ice crystals. Repeat this process two or three more times, until the ice cream is smooth but set. Cover with a tight-fitting lid and freeze until required.

MAKES ABOUT 1 LITRE (35 FL OZ/4 CUPS)

Lambic, a style of beer that originated in an area southwest of Brussels known as Pajottenland, is unique because the brewer allows the unfermented beer, known as wort, to be infected by wild yeast, and this can only be done from October to May when the weather conditions are right. The beer is then aged for one to three years before being blended with young lambic, bottled and sold as gueuze lambic. Gueuze can be described as being very tart, cidery, sweet, sour and dry all at the same time. Lambic is also used to make a fruit beer by adding fruit or fruit syrup to it and allowing a secondary fermentation. This is then bottled and sold according to the fruit used. Kriek lambic is made by using morello cherries in the fermenting process, thus giving the beer a sweet–sour cherry character. Other flavours include raspberry (framboise lambic) and blackcurrant (cassis lambic), among others.

Kriek lambic sorbet

165 g (5¾ oz/¾ cup) caster (superfine) sugar   500 ml (17 fl oz/2 cups) kriek lambic

Place the sugar and 125 ml (4 fl oz/½ cup) water in a saucepan over medium heat, stirring constantly without boiling until the sugar has dissolved. Turn up the heat, bring the syrup to the boil, then boil for 1 minute. Remove from the heat. Stir in the kriek lambic, then tip the mixture into a glass bowl or container with a lid and place in the freezer overnight.

The next day, use a fork to scrape the surface of the sorbet, breaking it up – it will not have frozen solid because of the sugar and alcohol content. Put the sorbet scrapings and chunks into a food processor and blitz until the sorbet is all broken up and the texture becomes silky, about 5 minutes or so.

Pour the mixture into a running ice-cream machine and churn for 20–30 minutes. Spoon into a container with a lid and freeze until you are ready to serve.

Alternatively, pour the mixture out of the food processor into a shallow tray and place in the freezer. Beat it vigorously once it has started to freeze, as this will break up the ice crystals. Repeat this three or four more times, until the sorbet is set, with no big ice crystals visible. Cover with a tight-fitting lid and freeze until required.

SERVES 6–8

The Hoegaarden Grand Cru is a big, sweet Belgian wheat ale coming in at 8.5 per cent alcohol. It has a lovely sweet, malt character, subtle wheat influence and spice notes from coriander (cilantro). Possessing a fruity/estery bite from the yeast and warmth from the high alcohol content, it is a great beer for making cakes and sweet rich sauces.

Sticky date pudding

250 g (9 oz/1⅓ cups) pitted dried dates
1 teaspoon bicarbonate of soda (baking soda)
250 ml (9 fl oz/1 cup) Hoegaarden Grand Cru
100 g (3½ oz) unsalted butter, softened
185 g (6½ oz/1 cup) brown sugar
1 teaspoon vanilla extract
2 free-range eggs
260 g (9¼ oz/1¾ cups) self-raising flour

HOEGAARDEN BUTTERSCOTCH SAUCE
500 ml (17 fl oz/2 cups) whipping cream
185 g (6½ oz/1 cup) brown sugar
60 g (2¼ oz) unsalted butter
80 ml (2½ fl oz/⅓ cup) Hoegaarden Grand Cru, or any of the beers suggested below

Preheat the oven to 180°C (350°F/Gas 4). Grease a 22 cm (8½ inch) springform cake tin and line it with baking paper.

Chop the dates in a blender, then place in a bowl and sprinkle with the bicarbonate of soda. In a saucepan, bring the beer and 125 ml (4 fl oz/½ cup) water to the boil, then pour over the dates and mix well. Leave to soak for 20–30 minutes.

Using electric beaters, cream the butter, sugar and vanilla in a bowl until pale and creamy. Add one egg and mix well, then add the second egg and mix it in well. Use a spatula to fold the date mixture through, then gently fold in the flour.

Spoon the batter into the cake tin, level the top and bake for about 1 hour, checking it after 50 minutes. The pudding is ready when a skewer inserted into the centre comes out clean. If the top browns a little too quickly, cover it with some foil. Remove from the oven.

When the pudding is nearly done, make the butterscotch sauce. Put the cream, sugar and butter in a saucepan and bring to the boil, then reduce the heat and simmer for about 8 minutes. Stir in the beer and simmer for a further 2–3 minutes.

Cut the pudding into slices or wedges, place on serving plates or in bowls and drench with the sauce. Serve with a scoop of vanilla ice cream – or even better, my wheat beer ice cream (see page 180)!

SERVES 6–8

BEER NOTES
Alternatives are other high-alcohol Belgian ales such as Westmalle Tripel, Rochefort 8 or 10, or of course a locally made big Belgian Trappist-style ale

Baking

We should all say a silent thanks to a truly remarkable living organism called *Saccharomyces cerevisiae*, for without it we wouldn't have bread or beer as we know them. Yes, for the last 5000 years this very clever little fella – otherwise known as yeast – has been responsible for converting the fermentable sugars found in bread dough and beer wort into carbon dioxide, which helps to create light, airy bread and nice, gassy beer. It is also responsible for creating the alcohol in our beer, which provides wonderful complex flavours – and using those flavours is what this book is all about. So what better way to pay homage to our yeasty friend than to combine the two ingredients it likes best – beer and flour – with a bunch of other delectable ingredients like apples, raisins, bananas, rhubarb, chocolate, spices, herbs, cheese, salami, or even some pumpkin, and bake them together until aromatic and golden. Some of these baked goodies are sweet and others are savoury, but I guarantee all of them are delicious!

Cinnamon, apple and saison muffins

1 large or 2 small granny smith apples
1 large or 2 small pink lady apples
150 g (5½ oz/1 cup) wholemeal (whole-wheat)
    self-raising flour
150 g (5½ oz/1 cup) self-raising flour
140 g (5 oz/¾ cup) brown sugar

1½ teaspoons ground cinnamon
¼ teaspoon ground nutmeg
125 g (4½ oz/½ cup) unsalted butter, melted
2 free-range eggs, lightly beaten
125 g (4½ oz/½ cup) plain yoghurt
185 ml (6 fl oz/¾ cup) Belgian ale

Preheat the oven to 180°C (350°F/Gas 4). Line two 12-hole standard muffin tins with paper cases.

Peel and core the apples and cut them into 4–5 mm (¼ inch) slices. Cut these into dice – if you like chunkier pieces of apple in your muffins, dice them larger. You will need 125 g (4½ oz/1 cup) of diced granny smith and 125 g (4½ oz/1 cup) of diced pink lady apple.

Put all the dry ingredients in a large mixing bowl and stir until well combined. In a separate bowl, thoroughly mix together the butter, eggs, yoghurt and beer, then mix the apples through.

Add the wet mixture to the dry mixture and use a spatula to combine all the ingredients, folding them just enough to bring the mixture together. Do not over-mix as this can result in tough muffins.

Divide the mixture evenly among the paper cases. Bake for 20–25 minutes, or until a skewer inserted into the centre of a muffin comes out clean. Turn the muffins out onto a wire rack to cool. They will last for 2–3 days in an airtight container.

MAKES 18

BEER NOTES
Try La Chouffe,
Saison Dupont,
Bridge Road
Brewers Chevalier
Saison, Otway
Estate or the Temple
Brewing Company

Chocolate stout brownies

125 g (4½ oz) unsalted butter, diced
150 g (5½ oz) good-quality milk chocolate,
    chopped
100 g (3½ oz) good-quality dark chocolate
    (75% cocoa), chopped
3 free-range eggs

100 g (3½ oz/½ cup) brown sugar
60 ml (2 fl oz/¼ cup) stout
125 g (4½ oz) plain (all-purpose) flour
2 tablespoons unsweetened cocoa powder
70 g (2½ oz/½ cup) chopped macadamia nuts
90 g (3¼ oz/½ cup) white chocolate chips

Preheat the oven to 180°C (350°F/Gas 4). Grease a 4 cm (1½ inch) deep, 20 cm (8 inch) square brownie or lamington tin and line it with baking paper.

Put the butter and all the chopped chocolate in a heatproof glass bowl. Place the bowl over a saucepan of gently simmering water, making sure the water does not touch the bottom of the bowl. Stir gently until all the ingredients are melted. Remove the bowl from the heat and set aside to cool while you beat the eggs.

Using electric beaters, whisk the eggs and sugar together in a bowl until light and fluffy, 10–15 minutes. Add the beer and mix again. Add the melted chocolate and mix thoroughly. Sift the combined flour and cocoa powder into the bowl and fold them through until well combined. Fold in the macadamia nuts and chocolate chips.

Pour the mixture into the prepared brownie tin, spreading it around evenly. Bake until set, about 15 minutes. Remove from the oven and cool on a wire rack before turning out. Cut into squares to serve.

MAKES 8–16 PIECES, DEPENDING ON HOW BIG YOU CUT THEM

BEER NOTES
Try Coopers Best
Extra Stout, Otway
Estate Prickly Moses
Stout, Moo Brew
Imperial Stout,
Southwark Old
Stout, Mountain
Goat Surefoot
Stout, Nail Brewing
Company Nail
Stout or Arctic Fox
Chocolate Stout

The German style of wheat beer is a wonderful, refreshing and unique ale. It is a yeast-driven beer, meaning that during the fermentation process the yeast gives the beer a lot of flavour characteristics, namely those of banana and cloves. These flavours work so well with the slight tart and sour character from the wheat and they make this beer great both to drink and to cook with.

Hefeweizen banana bread

300 g (10½ oz/2 cups) wholemeal (whole-wheat) self-raising flour

75 g (2½ oz/½ cup) plain (all-purpose) bread flour

140 g (5 oz/¾ cup firmly packed) brown sugar

125 g (4½ oz) unsalted butter, melted

2 free-range eggs, lightly beaten

80 g (2¾ oz/⅓ cup) sour cream

185 ml (6 fl oz/¾ cup) German wheat beer

180 g (6½ oz/¾ cup) mashed ripe banana (about 2 bananas)

TOPPING

60 g (2¼ oz/½ cup) slivered almonds

45 g (1½ oz/¼ cup) brown sugar

Preheat the oven to 180°C (350°F/Gas 4). Grease a 21 x 9 cm (8¼ x 3½ inch) loaf (bar) tin and line the base and two opposite sides with baking paper, allowing it to overhang.

Put the wholemeal flour, plain flour and sugar in a bowl and mix with electric beaters on low speed until combined. Add the butter, eggs, sour cream, beer and mashed banana and mix on medium–high speed for 3–5 minutes.

Pour the batter into the loaf tin and gently bang it on the work surface several times to level the mixture and set it in the tin. Combine the topping ingredients, then sprinkle a generous amount on top of the loaf. You will probably only need to use about three-quarters of the mixture, so I recommend that you eat the rest of it as it is simply delicious!

Put the bread in the oven, turn the temperature down to 170°C (325°F/Gas 3) and bake for 40 minutes.

Turn the tin around in the oven so that the bread cooks evenly, reduce the temperature to 160°C (315°F/Gas 2–3) and bake for another 45 minutes, or until a skewer inserted in the centre of the loaf comes out clean. Cool in the tin for 10 minutes, then turn the bread out and rest on a wire rack.

Eat the bread hot, or wait for it to cool down – either way it is delicious. The bread will keep for about 3 days in an airtight container.

MAKES 1 LOAF

BEER NOTES
For this recipe you could use a hefeweizen from brewers such as Erdinger, Schofferhofer or Franziskaner – or try a locally made version

My local bottle shop had just received a shipment of an imperial stout from Baird Brewing Company, a little micro-brewery in Japan, and after tasting it I thought it would be perfect in this cake ... and it is! So check out what's new in your bottle shop, or ask them to get this in. Otherwise, try a locally made imperial stout. A big beer with high alcohol, lots of malt complexity, malt sweetness and big hop bitterness, it is a great style to bake with!

Upside-down rhubarb stout cake

600 g (1 lb 5 oz) rhubarb (about 1½ bunches), chopped into 4 cm (1½ inch) lengths
150 g (5½ oz/¾ cup) caster (superfine) sugar
finely grated zest of 1 lemon
125 ml (4 fl oz/½ cup) imperial stout – try Dark Sky Imperial Stout (9%) from Japan – plus 2 tablespoons extra
125 g (4½ oz) unsalted butter, softened

185 g (6½ oz/1 cup) brown sugar
2 free-range eggs
175 g (6 oz/¾ cup) sour cream
150 g (5½ oz/1 cup) self-raising flour
150 g (5½ oz/1 cup) wholemeal (whole-wheat) flour
½ teaspoon ground cinnamon

Preheat the oven to 180°C (350°F/Gas 4). Grease a 24 cm (9½ inch) round cake tin and line the base and side with baking paper.

Put the rhubarb, caster sugar, lemon zest and the extra 2 tablespoons of beer in a saucepan. Stir over medium–high heat until the sugar has dissolved and the rhubarb is well coated. Turn the heat down to a simmer and gently cook for about 10 minutes, or until the rhubarb is just soft. Remove from the heat.

Using electric beaters, cream the butter and brown sugar in a bowl until smooth. Add one egg, mix until smooth, then add the other egg and mix until incorporated. Mix the sour cream through, and finally the 125 ml (4 fl oz/½ cup) of beer.

Sift the self-raising flour into a bowl and add the wholemeal flour and cinnamon. Stir together well, then fold through the wet ingredients until well combined.

Remove the rhubarb from the saucepan with a slotted spoon and transfer to the middle of the cake tin. Flatten it out to within 2 cm (¾ inch) of the side of the tin. Gently spoon in the batter, first filling in the gap between the rhubarb and the tin. Use a spatula to carefully spread the batter over the rhubarb and level the surface.

Bake for 45 minutes, or until a skewer inserted into the middle of the cake comes out clean. Remove from the oven, allow to cool for 30 minutes, then turn it out on to a plate. You can serve this cake warm or cold, with thick cream, ice cream or yoghurt, or just on its own. It will keep for 4–5 days in an airtight container.

SERVES 12

I know Anzac biscuits are traditionally made using golden syrup, but I thought I'd give them a slightly different slant and use maple syrup and a really nice hoppy ale. If you just can't bring yourself to make them without golden syrup, that's fine – go the gold.

Real ale Anzac biscuits

125 g (4½ oz/½ cup) unsalted butter
2 tablespoons maple syrup
3 tablespoons American-style pale ale
1 teaspoon bicarbonate of soda (baking soda)
150 g (5½ oz/1 cup) plain (all-purpose) flour

100 g (3½ oz/1 cup) rolled (porridge) oats
65 g (2¼ oz/¾ cup) desiccated (grated dried) coconut
140 g (5 oz/¾ cup lightly packed) brown sugar

Preheat the oven to 180°C (350°F/Gas 4). Grease two or three large baking trays or pizza trays.

Melt the butter in a saucepan over medium heat, add the maple syrup and beer and stir well to combine. Add the bicarbonate of soda, mix well, then remove from the heat.

In a large bowl, mix the flour, rolled oats, coconut and sugar until well combined. Add the butter mixture and stir until all the ingredients are completely combined.

Take a dessertspoon full of the mixture and roll it in the palm of your hand until you have a ball. Place this on one of the trays and flatten it slightly. Roll out the remaining mixture in the same way, placing about five balls on each tray, as you'll need to allow plenty of room for the biscuits to spread as they bake.

Bake each tray of biscuits for 10–15 minutes, or until golden, rotating the tray every 5 minutes or so to ensure even cooking. Bake the biscuits in batches if you don't have enough trays.

Remove the biscuits from the oven and leave to cool on the trays for 5 minutes before removing them, as they'll be quite soft straight out of the oven. The biscuits will keep well in an airtight container for many days.

MAKES ABOUT 20

BEER NOTES
American-style pale ales include Arctic Fox American Pale Ale, Stone & Wood Pacific Ale and Moo Brew Pale Ale

If you've never tried Timmermans Fruits de la Forêt lambic beer, you'll be blown away by its aroma and flavour. It is very sweet, very fruity and a real delight. I know it will be a little difficult to get, but the reward is well worth the effort as it adds a lovely subtle, fruity character to the scones. When you do buy the beer, buy a few bottles – one for the scones, one to drink and a couple to use in other recipes.

This is only one of many scone recipes we can make with beer. You could do a savoury scone with stout and goat's cheese, for instance. Go on – be inspired!

Really simple fruit-beer scones

300 g (10½ oz/2 cups) self-raising flour, plus
    75 g (2½ oz/½ cup) extra
1 tablespoon caster (superfine) sugar

185 ml (6 fl oz/¾ cup) Timmermans
    Fruits de la Forêt lambic
60 ml (2 fl oz/¼ cup) cream

Preheat the oven to 220°C (425°F/Gas 7) and line a baking tray with baking paper.

Sift the 300 g (10½ oz/2 cups) flour into a large bowl. Add the sugar, beer and cream and, using a butter knife or a spatula, 'cut' through the mixture until it is well combined. This will be a fairly wet mixture, so add some of the extra flour, a handful at a time, until the dough comes together and you are able to tip it out of the bowl onto a floured work surface. It may still be a little sticky, but that's okay. Give the dough a gentle knead until it feels smooth and silky, but do not overwork it or you'll end up with tough scones.

Using your hands, gently flatten the dough out to roughly a 2 cm (¾ inch) thickness, trying to keep it level. Using a circular biscuit (cookie) cutter or a small glass that has been dipped in flour, cut out as many scones as you can. Put them on the baking tray just lightly touching each other – this helps them rise evenly. When you can't cut out any more rounds, gently roll the dough scraps together, flatten it out again to about 2 cm (¾ inch) thick and cut out more rounds. Continue like this until all the dough has been used up.

Bake for 12–15 minutes, or until the scones are golden and have risen. To help them cook evenly, turn the tray around after the first 7 minutes. You can tell when the scones are cooked: they'll sound hollow when you gently tap them with your finger.

Serve warm, with jam and cream.

MAKES ABOUT 12

BEER NOTES
If you can't find the Fruits de la Forêt, use a kriek lambic, framboise lambic or a cassis lambic

Red Hill Brewery Scotch Ale is a malt-driven dark ale with quite a sweet character, which carries 5.8 per cent alcohol. Not many breweries in Australia are making a Scotch ale, which is a shame because it is a great style with a lovely complexity. The Red Hill Brewery Scotch Ale goes really well with the rosemary and ricotta cheese in this recipe. If you can't get a Scotch ale, go for a porter such as a Lord Nelson Old Admiral, or a stout such as Steam Exchange Brewery's Steam Exchange Stout.

Scotch ale and ricotta muffins

300 g (10½ oz/2 cups) self-raising flour
3 teaspoons chopped fresh rosemary
80 g (2¾ oz) unsalted butter, melted
140 g (5 oz/¾ cup) brown sugar

2 free-range eggs
250 g (9 oz/1 cup) ricotta cheese
250 ml (9 fl oz/1 cup) Red Hill Brewery Scotch Ale

Preheat the oven to 180°C (350°F/Gas 4). Either grease the holes of a standard 12-hole muffin tin, or line them with paper cases.

In a bowl, mix the flour, rosemary and a pinch of sea salt together. Put the remaining ingredients in another bowl and give them a really good mix to combine. Tip them into the flour bowl and fold through until combined – do not over-mix.

Divide the mixture evenly among the muffin holes, then bake for 15–20 minutes, or until a skewer inserted into the centre of a muffin comes out clean. Remove from the oven and allow to cool for 10 minutes, then turn out onto a wire rack.

You can eat these muffins warm or at room temperature, with or without butter – I prefer without. They will keep well for 3 days in an airtight container.

MAKES 12

Pumpkin damper

500 g (1 lb 2 oz) jap or kent pumpkin
(winter squash)
125 ml (4 fl oz/½ cup) Belgian ale, such as Duvel,
La Chouffe, Saison Dupont or Chimay Red

450 g (1 lb/3 cups) self-raising flour
1 teaspoon ground sage

Preheat the oven to 190°C (375°F/Gas 5) and line a baking tray with baking paper.

Peel the pumpkin, remove the seeds and cut the flesh into chunks. Place in a saucepan, cover with water, add a generous pinch of sea salt and bring to the boil. Cook until tender, then drain well. Push the pumpkin through a fine sieve, into a large mixing bowl. Add the beer and mix to combine well and form a liquid purée.

In a large bowl, mix together the flour, sage and a pinch of sea salt. Slowly mix in the pumpkin mixture until a nice dough forms – you may not need all the pumpkin purée for this.

Turn the dough out onto a floured work surface and give it a good kneading for 5–10 minutes, or until smooth and elastic. Form into a round loaf shape, place on the baking tray and spray with some water.

Bake for 30–40 minutes, or until a skewer inserted into the middle of the damper comes out clean. You will know it is cooked when you turn it over and tap the bottom and it sounds hollow.

Slice the damper and eat it on its own, either warm or at room temperature, with butter or with cream – your choice.

SERVES 8–10

Italian beer bread

1 tablespoon olive oil

a good of pinch of sugar

350 ml (12 fl oz) pilsner, heated to lukewarm

3 teaspoons dried yeast

650 g (1 lb 7 oz/4⅓ cups) plain (all-purpose)
   bread flour or 'oo' flour, plus extra, for flouring

1 teaspoon sea salt

60 g (2¼ oz/⅓ cup) pitted kalamata olives,
   roughly chopped

50 g (1¾ oz/⅓ cup) sun-dried tomatoes,
   chopped

40 g (1½ oz/⅓ cup) diced pecorino cheese
   (cut into 1 cm/½ inch cubes)

2 teaspoons chopped fresh rosemary

60 g (2¼ oz) piece of salami, pepperoni,
   sopressata or even capicola, cut into 1 cm
   (½ inch) cubes

BEER NOTES

Keeping with the Italian theme, I used Peroni Nastro Azzurro. Note that you'll need to buy two bottles of beer for this recipe, to get the right ratio of liquid to flour, but you will use only a small amount of the second bottle for the bread – so drink the rest instead!

Put the olive oil and sugar in a jug with the warm beer, then add the yeast. Give it a stir and let it sit for 10–15 minutes while the yeast gets itself going. It should develop a nice foamy head.

Put the flour in a large bowl and mix the salt through. Slowly add the yeast mixture and mix – either with your hands on a work surface, or in a mixer with a dough hook – until you get a ball of dough. If you need to add a little more liquid, add some warm water (or beer if you haven't already drunk the rest), to the jug that had the yeast in it. Swirl it around to pick up any leftover yeast and use that.

Turn the dough out onto a floured work surface and give it a good kneading for 10 minutes, or until you feel the consistency and texture change to a more smooth and silken feel.

Spray a large glass bowl with olive oil spray, then sprinkle flour inside so it sticks to the oil – this stops the dough sticking to the bowl while it rises. Put the dough in the bowl. Spray one side of a large sheet of plastic wrap with more oil and dust with flour. Cover the bowl with the plastic, sprayed side down. Put the bowl in a warm place and leave to rise until the dough has doubled in size, anything up to 3 hours.

Turn the dough out onto a floured work surface. Knock it back with your fist to knock the air out of it and deflate it, then flatten it. Sprinkle the rest of the ingredients on top, then give it a good kneading, making sure to evenly distribute the olives, tomatoes, cheese, rosemary and salami throughout the dough. Shape the dough into a rustic-looking loaf or ball (or put it into an oiled baking tin), place on a lightly oiled baking tray and let it prove again, until doubled in size – the second rising of the dough should take about half as long as the initial rising, say an hour or two.

Preheat the oven to 180°C (350°F/Gas 4). Put the dough in the oven and bake for 35–45 minutes, or until done. You can tell when it is cooked by flicking the bottom of the loaf with your finger: if it sounds hollow, it is cooked.

MAKES 1 LOAF

Trappist beers are high-alcohol, full-bodied, complex, fruity ales brewed by Trappist monks. There are only seven Trappist breweries in the world – six in Belgium and one in the Netherlands. They have a fantastic history and brew some of the world's greatest beers. Westmalle commenced brewing in 1836, Westvleteren in 1838, Chimay 1863, Koningshoeven 1884, Rochefort 1899, Orval 1931 and Achel 1998 – although Achel's history traces back to 1648. These beers are also great to cook with.

Trappist fruit cake

125 g (4½ oz) unsalted butter, chopped
185 g (6½ oz/1 cup) brown sugar
375 g (13 oz) dried fruit medley
100 g (3½ oz) dried cranberries
50 g (1¾ oz) semi-dried figs, chopped quite small
¼ teaspoon ground cinnamon
¼ teaspoon ground nutmeg
¼ teaspoon ground cardamom
¼ teaspoon ground allspice

1 teaspoon bicarbonate of soda (baking soda)
60 ml (2 fl oz/¼ cup) sherry
250 ml (9 fl oz/1 cup) Belgian Trappist ale, such as Rocheforte 10 (11.3%) – I like the extra kick the high alcohol content of this beer gives!
2 free-range eggs, lightly beaten
100 g (3½ oz/¾ cup) macadamia nuts, chopped
150 g (5½ oz/1 cup) plain (all-purpose) flour
150 g (5½ oz/1 cup) self-raising flour

Preheat the oven to 160°C (315°F/Gas 2–3). Grease a 22 cm (8½ inch) springform cake tin and line the base and sides with baking paper, allowing the paper to rise 2.5 cm (1 inch) higher than the rim of the tin.

Put the butter, sugar, dried fruits, spices, bicarbonate of soda, sherry and beer in a large saucepan over medium–high heat. Stir so that all the ingredients are well combined, then bring the mixture to the boil. Remove from the heat and stir again to ensure the butter and sugar are melted. Pour the mixture into a large bowl and place it in the fridge to cool it down. Once the mixture is lukewarm, add the eggs and nuts and mix them through.

Put all the flour in a bowl and stir to combine. Fold the flour through the fruit until well incorporated. Spoon the batter into the cake tin and bake for 1½ hours, or until a skewer inserted into the middle of the cake comes out clean. Remove from the oven, carefully remove the springform ring and sit the cake on a wire rack.

Allow the cake to cool for a few hours – if you cut it before it has cooled it can crumble. Although this is a full-flavoured and dense cake similar to a Christmas cake, it does not have the shelf life of a Christmas cake. Tightly wrapped in foil, the cake will keep for a week, in theory – but it won't last that long as it is delicious.

SERVES 16

Index

Acknowledgments

There are many people who have helped me put this book together, and without their help I could not have done it. I am very proud of this book and also of all of the people who have helped to bring it into your hands. So to everyone at Murdoch Books, I say thank you. To Kylie Walker and Janine Flew for guiding me through the process, for giving me the good and the bad feedback and ultimately coming around to the idea that beer truly is a fabulous ingredient. To Hugh Ford for the wonderful design, look and feel of the book. To the recipe testers Grace Campbell, Joanne Glynn and Nick Eade; to Kirsty Sands and Caroline Jones for cooking at the photoshoot; to Cherise Pagano for styling the food; and to Julie Renouf for the wonderful photos – thank you all. Thanks also to Dave, Cam and the crew at Mountain Goat Brewery for allowing us to shoot there.

I want to thank my two youngest daughters: Emily for her constant encouragement and positivity, and Erin for taking all the cakes, muffins and scones I made to school to share with her school buddies – who actually loved them, by the way. I want to thank my long-suffering wife Andrea for eating every dish in this book and liking nearly all of them. Asking me 'What's for dinner?' was always a daunting experience for her, as invariably the answer was beer. Thank you for putting up with my mad, weird and strange obsession with cooking with beer and the dishes that I served you. Thank you for dipping your finger in the sauce almost every time I asked you to taste and for giving me your honest feedback about the flavours and balance of the 100 or so dishes that I cooked for you while writing this book. Thank you also for insisting on drinking wine with every meal I served up to you, thus proving that wine goes perfectly well with the fine recipes in this book.

My greatest debt of gratitude I hold for my eldest daughter, Elise. She really was my rock, my assistant and my teacher, especially when it came to baking. She cooked with me, argued with me, got fed up with me, supported me, inspired me and very rarely washed up. Thank you, my gorgeous daughter, for being my faithful assistant, companion and supporter during the journey of making the recipes that are in this book. I know secretly you think this is actually your book – and truth be told it is *our* book, as I couldn't have done it without you.

Lastly thank you to the brewers of the world, for without your inspiration, ingenuity and hard work I wouldn't have had anything to cook with.

Published in 2011 by Murdoch Books Pty Limited

Murdoch Books Australia
Pier 8/9
23 Hickson Road
Millers Point NSW 2000
Phone: +61 (0) 2 8220 2000
Fax: +61 (0) 2 8220 2558
www.murdochbooks.com.au
info@murdochbooks.com.au

Murdoch Books UK Limited
Erico House, 6th Floor
93–99 Upper Richmond Road
Putney, London SW15 2TG
Phone: +44 (0) 20 8785 5995
Fax: +44 (0) 20 8785 5985
www.murdochbooks.co.uk
info@murdochbooks.co.uk

For Corporate Orders & Custom Publishing contact Noel Hammond,
National Business Development Manager Murdoch Books Australia

Publisher: Kylie Walker
Designer: Hugh Ford
Photographer: Julie Renouf
Stylist: Cherise Pagano
Project Editor: Janine Flew
Editor: Katri Hilden
Production: Renee Melbourne

Text © Paul Mercurio 2011
The moral right of the author has been asserted.
Design © Murdoch Books Pty Limited 2011
Photography © Julie Renouf 2011

National Library of Australia Cataloguing-in-Publication Data

Author: Mercurio, Paul, 1963—
Title: Cooking with beer / Paul Mercurio.
ISBN: 978-1-74196-845-3 (pbk.)
Notes: Includes index.
Subjects: Cooking (Beer). Beer.
Dewey Number: 641.623

A catalogue record for this book is available from the British Library.

Printed by 1010 Printing International Limited, China. Reprinted 2011 (twice), 2012.

IMPORTANT: Those who might be at risk from the effects of salmonella poisoning (the elderly, pregnant women, young
children and those suffering from immune deficiency diseases) should consult their doctor with any concerns about eating
raw eggs.

CONVERSION GUIDE: You may find cooking times vary depending on the oven you are using. For fan-forced ovens, as a
general rule, set the oven temperature to 20°C (35°F) lower than indicated in the recipe. We have used 20 ml (4 teaspoon)
tablespoon measures. If you are using a 15 ml (3 teaspoon) tablespoon, add an extra teaspoon for each tablespoon speci-
fied. We have used 60 g (Grade 3) eggs in all recipes.